Buying and Caring for a Horse or Pony

Originally published in two volumes as *Buying and Keeping a Horse or Pony* and *Caring for a Horse or Pony* in 1976, and now revised into one comprehensive book, *Buying and Caring for a Horse or Pony* tells the first-time pony owner everything he or she needs to know about the care of the animal. Set out in question-and-answer form, the book covers all the myriad problems and queries of the novice owner, from how to find and buy a suitable pony in the first place through types and breeds, points of the horse, stabling, grazing, feeding, health, tack and equipment, to a useful glossary of terms. There are lots of useful diagrams and photographs to amplify the clear and concise text, and the book will provide an ideal handbook for the young pony owner.

'The first two books in the Young Riders Guides should find their way into the pocket of any boy or girl who has been inspired by an elementary guide to horse management.' (Margery Fisher in *Growing Point*).

Robert Owen has written many books on riding and horse management, some with John Bullock. He is a British Show Jumping Association judge and an active member of the British Horse Society, and lives in Surrey, where he devotes as much time as possible to instructing young riders. John Bullock has over forty years' experience of looking after and schooling horses of all kinds, from polo ponies to hunters. He is a District Commissioner for the Pony Club and lives in Wiltshire.

Acknowledgements

The photographs in this book were supplied by Equestrian (Press and General) Services Limited except the following:

British Spotted Horse and Pony Society:	page 45
Clive Hiles:	pages 42, 120
Irish Tourist Board:	page 26
Leslie Lane AIIP:	pages 28, 30, 34, 35, 36, 37, 39, 40, 41
Montague Lewis:	page 32
Photonews:	pages 18, 25, 44, 87
Pony and Light Horse:	pages 29, 33
Thomas A. Wilkie:	page 10

Buying and Caring for a Horse or Pony

Robert Owen and John Bullock

Beaver Books

A Beaver Original
Published by Arrow Books Limited
17-21 Conway Street, London W1P 6JD

A division of the Hutchinson Publishing Group

London Melbourne Sydney Auckland
Johannesburg and agencies throughout
the world

First published in 1976 in two volumes
under the titles *Buying and Keeping a Horse or Pony*
and *Caring for a Horse or Pony*

This combined and revised edition published in 1984

Illustrations by Gwen Green and Michael Youens

Set in Linotron Univers Light

Printed and bound in Great Britain by
Anchor Brendon Ltd, Tiptree, Essex

ISBN 0 09 935780 1

Contents

Buying a horse or pony

How does one go about buying a horse or pony?
Let us examine four of the ways open to us when we set about the task of finding a suitable pony to buy: going to a horse sale, answering advertisements, buying through a horse dealer, or buying a pony already known to you.

These two animals, both well presented, show clearly the difference between a horse and pony.

Buying at a horse sale

In the British Isles and, indeed, throughout the world, the Horse Sale is the traditional place at which to buy and sell. Such sales are advertised, and may take place weekly on normal 'market' days, or they may be held occasionally at local cattle markets. In the

Interest is being shown at the ringside for this pony 'under offer'. The auctioneer is asking for bids, and the pony will shortly be changing ownership. This scene is typical of many rural horse sales; it is a scene repeated frequently in countries throughout the world.

specialist equestrian magazines and sometimes in the national press you can find a Horse Sale advertised to take place at a farm or riding establishment or even at a racecourse. And these sales will be conducted under the watchful eye of an experienced and qualified auctioneer.

A list or catalogue of the horses and ponies being offered for sale will be made available a few weeks before the given date. In the catalogue will be found the conditions of sale and the details of warranty and soundness of the stock being offered. It is a good idea to study these conditions most carefully. You will, of course, need a trailer or horse box to take home any horse or pony you buy. Or you might be able to arrange for a local contractor to do this for you.

Particular breeds of pony may be offered for sale during the autumn months. These sales usually take place in the region where the breed originated. The ponies being sold at these sales may have been brought in from running free, but most likely they will be from established breeders.

Buying through advertisements

We have found that one of the most satisfactory ways to buy is through answering one or other of the hundreds of advertisements which offer horses and ponies for sale in the equestrian press. In Great Britain, one of the best-known and authoritative of all equestrian journals is the weekly *Horse and Hound.*

Once having made contact with the seller, either by letter or by telephone, and having arranged a date on which it is convenient to meet, you can go with the assurance that on what you have heard the breed or type, height and age, colour and markings are what you are wanting, since all this will have been discussed before you leave your home. When you meet the seller, and see and judge the horse he has on offer, you can make your decision in leisurely and congenial surroundings.

The advertisements use a variety of different phrases – all of which you will need to understand if you feel any is worth following up and the journey you will have to make to see what is being offered is to be worthwhile.

Some ponies are advertised as being 'bomb-proof'! And that can mean almost anything! It might indicate that the pony is so docile it is hardly a ride; or it might mean the owners have had it for a long time and, having got used to them and their ways, the pony *appears* to do nothing wrong. But, beware! Being bomb-proof does not mean the pony will never bolt or become excited.

From the pages of *Horse and Hound*

Horses are frequently advertised as being 'not a novice ride'. This can sometimes be read as a horse that is a somewhat difficult proposition, and is not for the inexperienced. Certainly not for someone buying for the first time! Neither will this type of horse be likely to give much peace of mind to the parent or to the rider.

But having said this, most advertisements do give a clear and honest indication of the horse or pony being offered. Do find out all you can before you set off to see the animal; make your judgement; see the horse or pony being ridden and then, if the animal is large enough, ride it yourself. And, always insist that your veterinary surgeon must carry out an examination before you will finally buy.

Buying through a dealer

A horse dealer makes his living by being able to find out what his customers require. Very, very few dealers live up to the bad reputation which has been given them in various books and films. If you really know exactly what you require you can go to a horse dealer and have the pleasure of being able to see a number of animals from which to select in any large dealer's yard. No dealer will ever insist you buy what he has found for you – especially if it is not all that you had hoped for.

Buying a pony known to you

This might have been headed 'Buying from a friend', though that would not be exactly what we mean! Ponies come on to the market for several reasons, one of which is that the rider has outgrown the mount. In this case owners love to know just who will be buying, and if you are known to them, so much the better. Perhaps a pony, well known to you at local shows, is one that you will have ridden – especially if it is owned by a friend. You will know something about it, something of how it performs, and quite a lot about its temperament – all valid reasons to take into account.

Knowledgeable friends and other people such as the District Commissioner of your local Branch of the Pony Club will always be available to give their help and guidance.

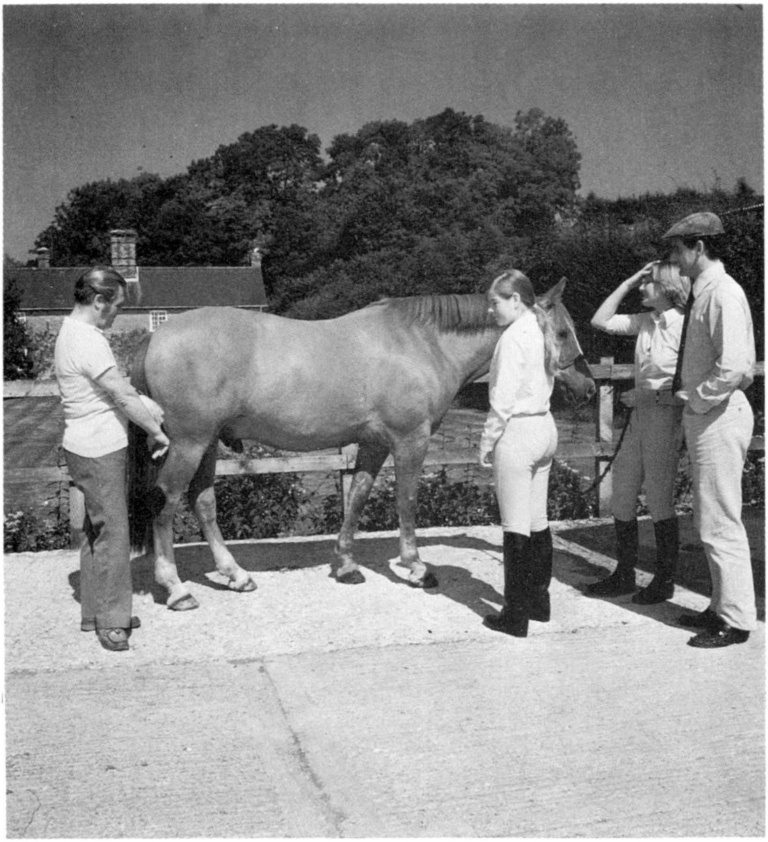

What is a pony?

Years ago people talked of ponies as being simply small horses. But this is not how we think today. Throughout the world the several different breeds of pony are recognised as being peculiar to a special location or a region, or to the part of the world in which that particular breed thrives.

It is as a result of selective breeding and the protection of certain characteristics that ponies today can be seen as part of the one species, *Equus caballus*, meaning the immediate forerunner of the modern horse.

The official definition of a pony is that it is a horse not standing over 14·2 hands. This will show how complicated it is when we try in a few words to make clear the differences between a pony and a horse!

On pages 28-41 details are given of the nine British native ponies. Today, the Breed Societies, the bodies which do so much to maintain the true characteristics of the breed, register pure-bred ponies in the Stud Books and Supplementary Registers. Other bodies, such as the National Pony Society, Ponies of Britain and the British Show Pony Society, set the standards by which the various breeds are judged.

The Shetland is one of the smallest of pony breeds.

This lovely pony has won two rosettes for its young riders.

What must be considered before buying a pony?

This is a most difficult question to answer, since there are so many factors which must come into the reckoning. For example, you will face a different series of problems if you are keeping a pony in the middle of a town, from someone who is keeping a pony in the country. Test yourself – see if you can give a 'yes' to the following:

1 Have you had some experience in looking after a pony?

2 Have you helped at a riding school? Or looked after a pony belonging to a friend?

3 Do you understand the responsibility you take on once you have a pony of your own?

4 Have you learned to ride well?

5 Have you joined the Pony Club or other riding organisation?

6 Are you sure you have the use of sufficient grazing land? And is this land really suitable for a pony?

7 Do you know what is meant by 'supplementary feeding'?

8 Are you prepared to read and learn all you can about keeping ponies; to take advice from those who have experience; and to spend each day the time which is so necessary to see that your pony, whether grass-kept or stable-kept, is well cared for?

Is there a rough guide to help find the right size of pony?

Certainly, there can be no firm and sure guide! Young people vary in height and weight, and to lay down a hard and fast rule that someone who is eight years old should 'fit' a 12·2 hands pony would be ridiculous. In any case, it would also depend on whether or not the eight-year-old had any experience of riding, and what was being asked of the pony.

On page 24 we show how ponies are measured and, provided a young person is of average height and build, the following would be a *very rough* guide.

height of pony	**approximate age of rider**
under 11 hands	under 7 years
between 11 and 12·2 hands	between 7 and 9 years
between 12·2 and 13·2 hands	between 9 and 12 years
between 13·2 and 14·2 hands	between 12 and 14 years
between 14·2 and 15·2 hands	between 14 and 16 years

If you look at the two ponies and riders pictured on the left you can see clearly that one pony is much too small for its rider and the other is too big. The pony and rider on this page are well matched.

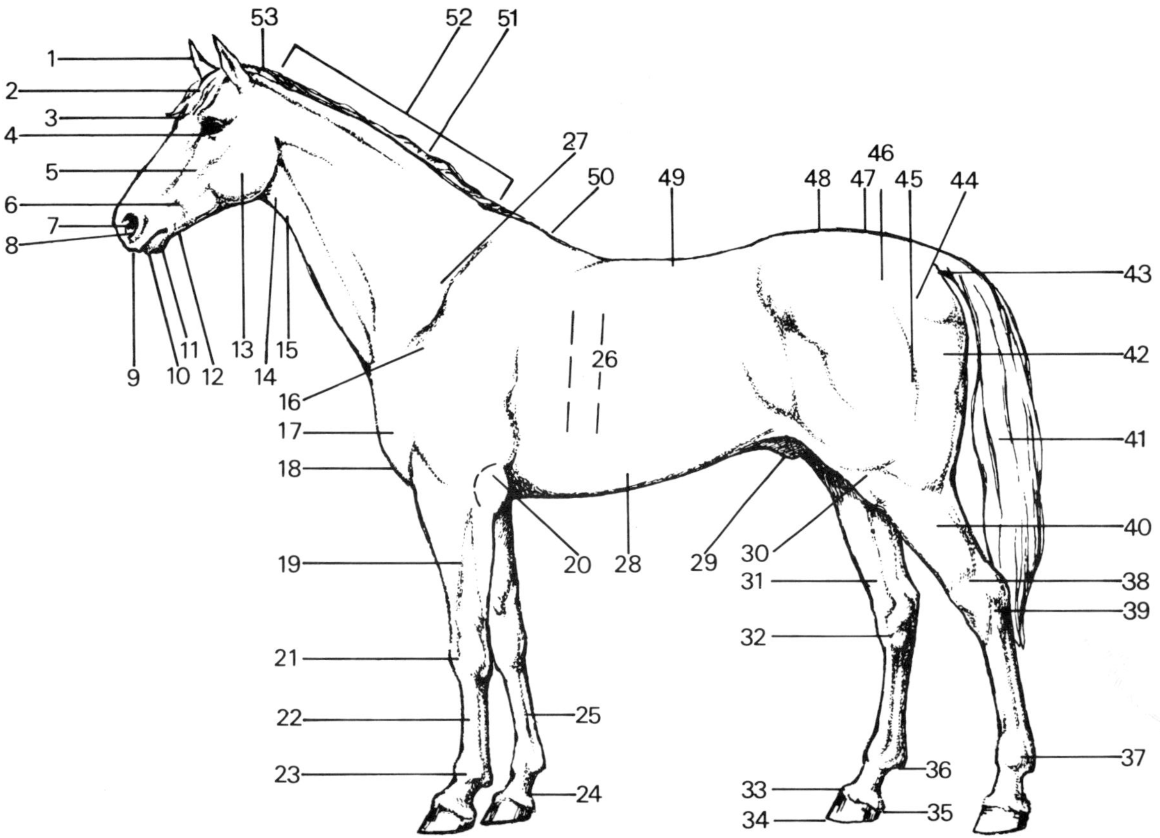
1
2
3
4
5
6
7
8
9
10
11
12
13
14
15
16
17
18
19
20
21
22
23
24
25
26
27
28
29
30
31
32
33
34
35
36
37
38
39
40
41
42
43
44
45
46
47
48
49
50
51
52
53

What are the points of a horse?

One of the first things you must learn are the names and positions given to the 'points' of a horse or pony. Unless these are recognised by you it will be difficult to discuss many aspects of equestrianism or to follow the information to be found in books of instruction. The points will also be used when deciding on what you should be looking for when choosing a horse or pony, and when talking with your veterinary surgeon.

But, even when you know the names of all the points, you will still find there is much to learn!

The points shown on the facing page are some of those you will most frequently use. More advanced books and manuals will give longer lists.

1 Ear
2 Forelock
3 Forehead
4 Eye
5 Cheekbone
6 Lower jaw
7 Nostril
8 Muzzle
9 Upper lip
10 Lower lip
11 Chin groove
12 Bars of jaw
13 Cheek
14 Gullet
15 Trachea (windpipe)
16 Point of shoulder
17 Breast
18 Pectoral muscle
19 Forearm
20 Elbow
21 Knee
22 Cannon bone
23 Fetlock joint
24 Pastern
25 Tendons
26 Girth
27 Base of neck
28 Belly
29 Sheath
30 Stifle
31 Shin
32 Chestnut
33 Coronet
34 Hoof (wall of foot)
35 Heel
36 Ergot
37 Fetlock
38 Hock
39 Point of hock
40 Gaskin
41 Tail
42 Buttocks
43 Dock
44 Hip joint
45 Thigh
46 Quarter
47 Croup
48 Point of croup
49 Back
50 Withers
51 Mane
52 Crest
53 Poll

Haroun, owned by the Tollard Park Arabian Stud, who was male champion Arab in England in 1974.

What is conformation?

This word is constantly used when discussing horses and ponies. It means, in very simple terms, the way the animal is 'put together'. Dictionaries tell us that the word conformation means form or shape – and that is a very good definition for our purposes.

A horse or pony with *good* conformation is well put together and of pleasing overall proportions. Even to an unskilled eye it is not difficult to recognize a horse with good conformation: the head, with clear and well-set eyes and neck, should neither be too large nor too small, and should be set on to good shoulders; the back must be straight, ending with strong hindquarters; the ribs and girth should be wide and large enough to house good lungs, and the legs firm and straight.

Look closely at the Arab horse in the photograph above. This picture shows good conformation. Now compare this with the drawing opposite. Here we have asked our artist to draw the sort of horse you *must* avoid – here is nothing but bad conformation!

Since when beginning we can never get our ideal, we should be satisfied if the animal we want to buy has some measure of good conformation. But never buy a badly 'put together' animal.

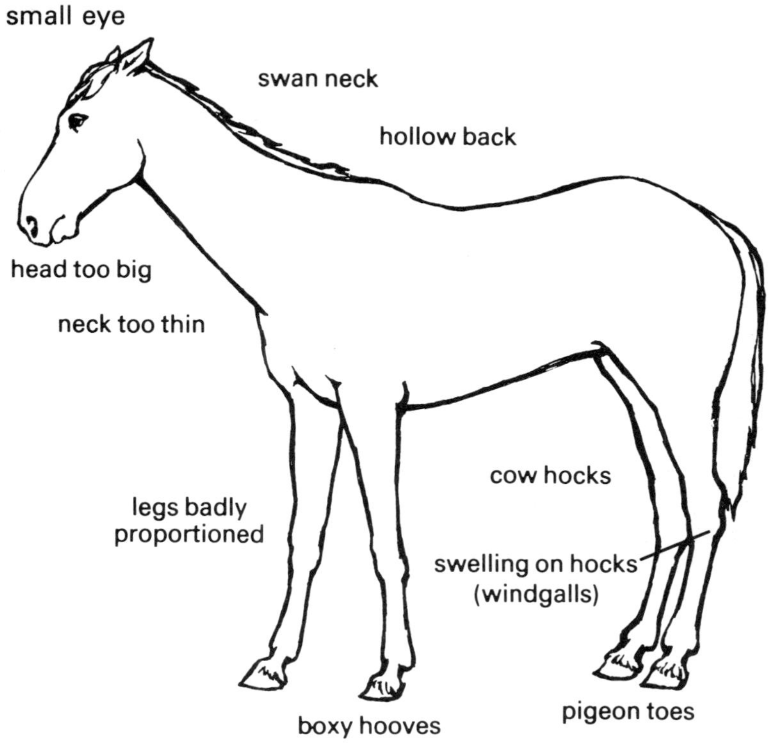

Points of conformation

Head Must be in good proportion to the overall look of the horse or pony. The bone structure should be well defined.
Eyes Should be kind, prominent and widely set.
Ears Should be set wide and forward and show alertness.
Neck Neither too long nor too short and set well into shoulders.
Shoulders Sloping in a line from the withers to the point of the shoulder.
Back Must blend with front and hindquarters. A short back is considered best, but this must show good proportions overall.
Hindquarters Clean and muscular.
Legs Square and solid in stance. Forelegs when seen from the front to be straight. Viewed from behind the legs must be straight and perpendicular to the body. There must be no puffy joints.
Pasterns Neither too large nor too short.
Hoofs Rounded and 'clean'.

What should one look out for when trying a pony?

When you see a likely pony, there are several things to watch out for:

1 If the pony is not in the field when you arrive, why not? Maybe it is difficult to catch.

2 Can a child put the saddle and bridle on unaided, and mount unaided either from the ground or a bank or bale of straw? If the pony won't stay still and allow a child to deal with it itself, you are buying yourself a full-time job.

3 Will the pony do as it is asked in its home surroundings without trying to dodge out of it and get back to its friends or own stable? If it tries to assert its own will this is known as being 'nappy', a most undesirable characteristic for a child's pony.

4 Is it really foolproof with traffic, especially big lorries? To buy a pony nowadays which is not 100% reliable with traffic is madness, and you will never have a moment's peace of mind if you do.

5 Does it look animated and happy, with ears pricked, or are the ears back showing signs of a nasty temperament? A bad or nervy temperament can never be wholly cured, especially by a child, because another child has probably caused it, through ignorance, in the first place.

6 No doubt you will have been told the age, but it is as well to be able to check this for yourself. A horse's age is shown by its teeth, and if you study the drawings on page 23, you should be able to get some idea for yourself. After the age of eight a horse is said to be 'aged', and then the development of the teeth may vary, and the exact age is difficult to determine.

7 Will the pony walk quietly and willingly into a horse box or trailer? This is known as 'quiet to box'. If not, you may well let yourself in for a lot of frustration and trouble because probably before long you will want to move somewhere beyond hacking distance.

(Reprinted by kind permission from *Keeping a Pony* by Jane and Melinda St Clair)

What is a 'vet's certificate'?

Before buying a horse or pony it is most strongly recommended that you first obtain your own veterinary surgeon's report. And *always* go by what he says! Even the most experienced of horsemen will never consider paying for a horse or pony until an examination has been undertaken, and until the report shows the animal is satisfactory. A vet's certificate will also be necessary if you approach an insurance company for insurance cover against the animal's illness, accident or death.

A vet's certificate will, if the animal is sound, give the correctly measured height, the age of the horse or pony, and something to the effect that an examination has been satisfactorily carried out, and that the horse or pony is sound, as far as the vet can judge, in wind and limb. A more advanced examination can be given, when the vet will use X-rays and other medical aids.

The examination given by a veterinary surgeon will cover the breathing and lung action of a horse, the heart and pulse rate, both when quiet and after having been galloped, an investigation of the eyes and a general examination of the head, a close look at the legs to check for splints, etc., and a check of the feet. He will also want to check the horse's action at the walk, trot and canter (see below).

How does one tell the age of a pony?

A pony's age is found by looking closely at his teeth. Different marks and shapes occur on the teeth at varying ages, though when a horse or pony reaches the age of eight years it becomes more difficult to be absolutely certain of age.

To examine the teeth first open the pony's mouth. To do this you use both hands, one for the upper lip and one for the lower. Do not hold too tightly on to the pony's jaw, but gently put your thumb and forefinger on to the bars of his lower jaw between the incisor teeth and molars (see the illustrations below).

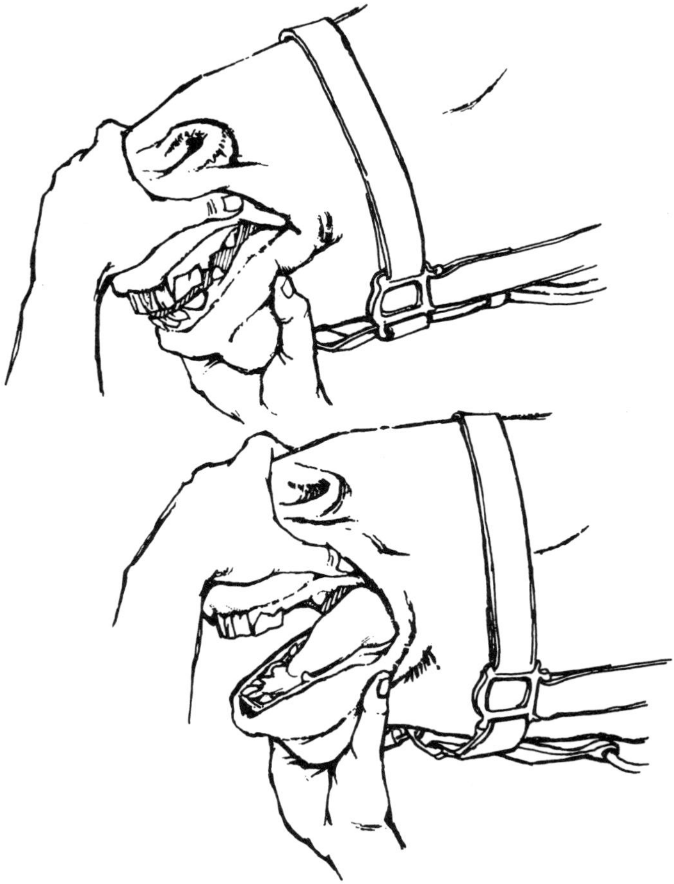

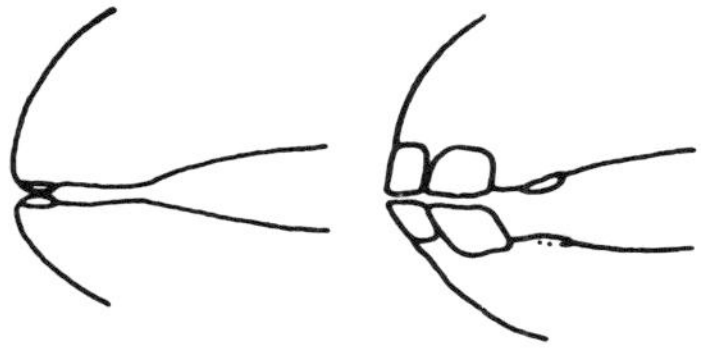

Birth to 6 months: The temporary incisors or milk teeth begin to appear after 10 days.

2 years: There is now a full set of milk teeth, showing small dark rings on the biting edges.

3 years: First permanent teeth. At first they show no marks, but these soon appear.

5 years: A 'full mouth' of permanent teeth. Corner incisors meet only at the front.

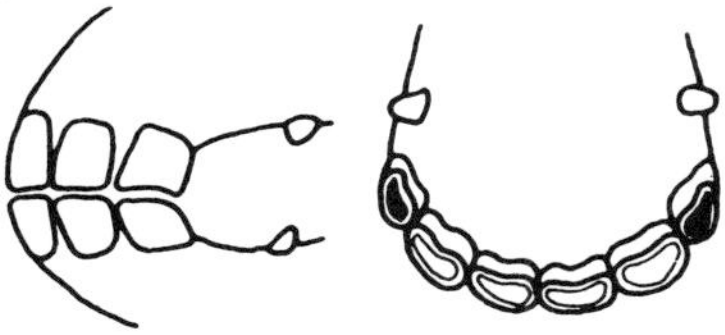

7 years: Corner incisors now meet, and a small hook appears on the upper corner incisors.

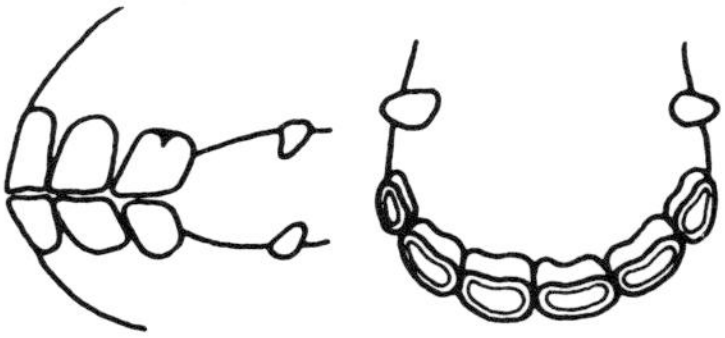

9 years: 'Galvayne's Groove' appears at top corner incisors. At this age it is about 3 mm ($^{1}/_{8}$ inch) long.

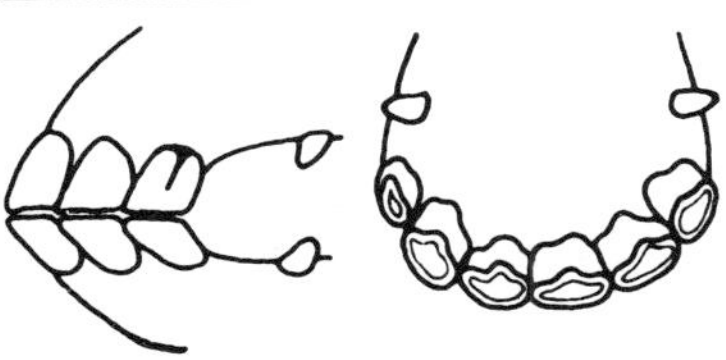

15 years: Teeth have become more triangular and are beginning to slope out.

25 years: Slope of incisors is very pronounced. Galvayne's Groove is disappearing.

How are ponies measured?

The height of a pony is the measurement found when taking the line from the ground to the highest part of the withers. In English-speaking countries measurement is given in hands and inches, each hand being 4 inches (10 cm). This somewhat peculiar and, in the early days, not very accurate measure came from what was thought to be the width of an average man's hand.

Other countries today give and record height measurements only in metres and centimetres.

The main characteristics of many breeds are determined by height, and the height of a pony will also determine into which class or event it may compete or be shown at a horse show. Therefore it becomes increasingly important to have some accurate record of the height of a pony.

The true measurement is taken when a pony is standing on level ground; allow 1·25 cm (1/2 inch) for the shoe if the pony is shod.

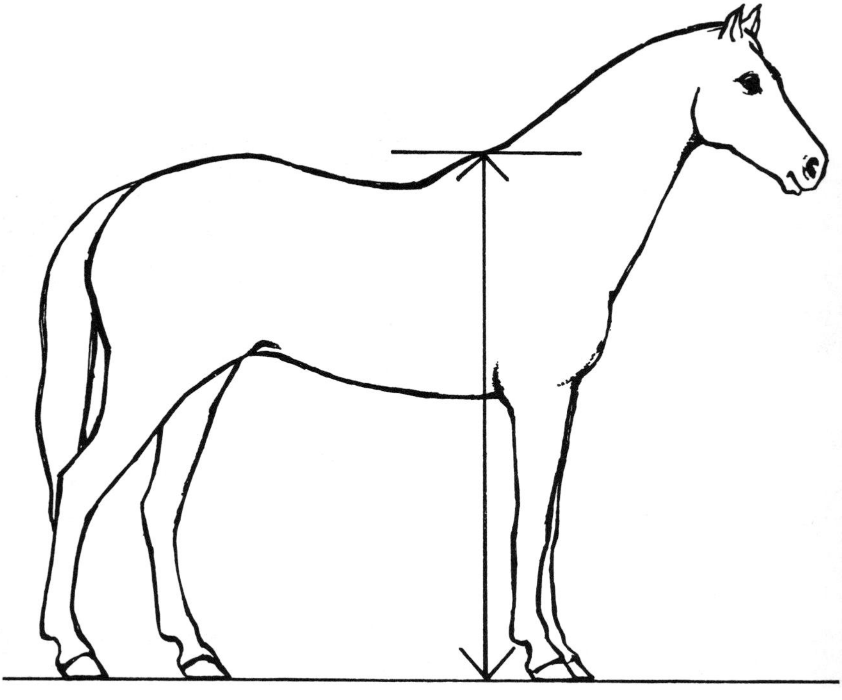

Breeds

What are mountain and moorland ponies?

These are the breeds which are known as 'British Native Ponies'. The nine types can be grouped into three regional sections: the northern group, comprising the Highland, Dales and Fell; the western group, comprising the Welsh and the Connemara from Ireland; the southern group, comprising the Dartmoor, Exmoor and New Forest. By itself, though very much part of the northern group, is the Shetland – the smallest of all the mountain and moorland ponies.

Each of the native breeds has inherited wonderful qualities. They are ideal for living out at grass, they are extremely hardy, and they make excellent riding ponies and ponies from which to breed. Competitions are held at many shows throughout the world which seek best of breed. A description and photograph of each of the British native breeds are given on the following pages.

Connemara ponies in their natural environment

In addition to the British native pony breeds we shall be discussing in the next few pages, there are several breeds which are equally well-known in their own countries. These include the Fjord, Icelandic, Falabella, Barthais, Dulmen and the different breeds in Australia, New Zealand and elsewhere.

1 Highland
2 Dales
3 Fell
4 Welsh
5 Connemara
6 Dartmoor
7 New Forest
8 Exmoor
9 Shetland

The Highland pony

The Highland is one of the largest and strongest of the native pony breeds and is found in the highlands of Scotland and in some of the outer islands. There are two main types: those who live and thrive on the mainland and who stand between 13·2 hands and 14·2 hands; and those found on the islands – a smaller breed standing between 12·2 hands and 13·2 hands. The larger breed are sometimes referred to as 'Mainland' ponies.

These are ideal as riding ponies and are used extensively for trekking and hill climbing.

A certain amount of foreign blood has been introduced, much of which is Arab, and the Highland is also a good, honest working pony used for carrying loads for the crofters. They are extremely healthy and strong, surviving throughout the year on some of the toughest country and in the severest of weather conditions.

Description *Height* Between 13·2 hands and 14·2 hands *Colours* Black, brown with occasional dun and grey. No white markings

Head Well carried, attractive *Ears* Short and well set *Neck* Strong and not over-pronounced *Back, loins and quarters* Short back with a slight curve. Powerful quarters and loins *Tail* Strong and well set on, carried gaily, with a plentiful covering of hair almost reaching the ground

Breed Society The Highland Pony Society

The Dales pony

Like the Fells, the Dales are natives of the northern part of England. For centuries they have lived between the Pennine Chain of hills to the west and the coastline of Durham and Yorkshire to the east. Another similarity to the Fells is that they also were used to carry lead from the mining areas to the ports along the north-east coast.

The Dales are generally larger than the Fell ponies, usually standing well up to 14·2 hands. They are the heaviest and perhaps strongest of all the British native breeds. The breed has immense stamina and always has good legs and feet.

Today the Dales are found mainly in Durham, Northumberland and parts of Yorkshire and, although appearing more frequently in the show rings, the breed is ideal for the growing demand for ponies suitable for trekking and trail riding. They are quiet and gentle and are able to carry a full-grown person all day in the fells. In fact, it is claimed that the Dales, once broken, are capable of doing all the work required on a small farm.

Description *Colours* Many are black, though there are bays, browns and greys *Head* A neat head, well balanced with the overall conformation of the breed *Ears* Small and neatly set *Back, loins and quarters* Strong and full *Tail* Modest and carried rather low *Feet* Good feet and well feathered heels
Breed Society The Dales Pony Society

Fell pony

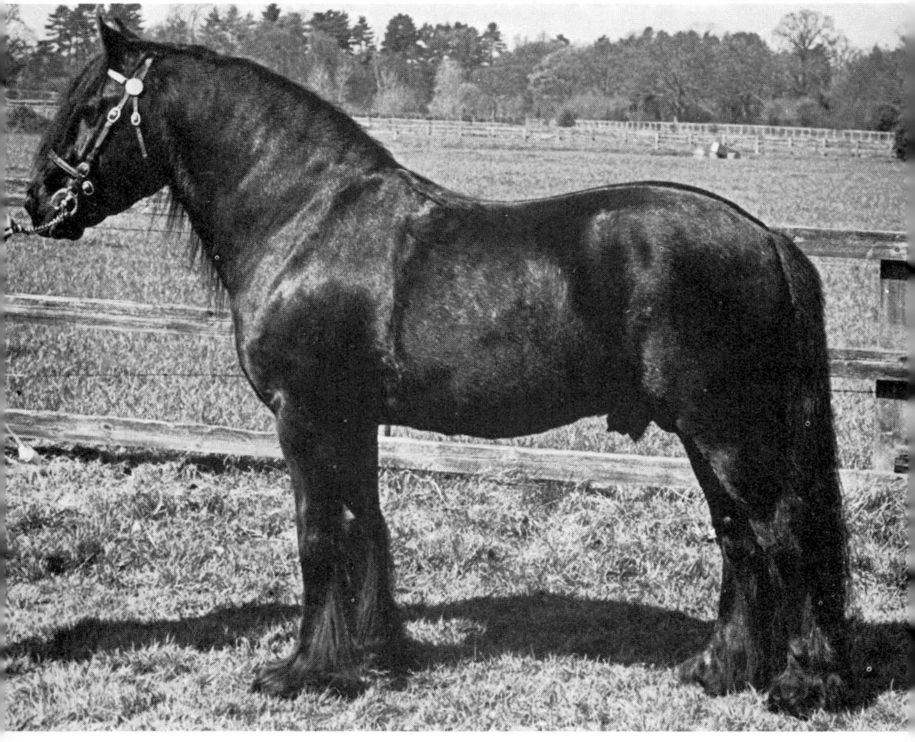

The Fell pony

The Fell pony is a breed peculiar to Cumbria, formerly comprising the counties of Cumberland and Westmorland. This area, bordering on the Lake District, is in the north-west corner of England, its eastern flank being the Pennines which run from north to south for a distance of nearly 300 miles.

The Fell is a strong and powerfully built pony, used in the seventeenth, eighteenth and early nineteenth centuries to carry heavy loads of lead from the mines to the ports on the north-eastern coastline. These heavy loads were taken on routes over the Pennines and across the bleakness of Westmorland and Durham. Many of the pack trails still remain.

As with all the British native breeds, the Fell pony is an excellent riding pony, standing usually about 13·2 hands. The breed has been developed into a highly-prized show pony, though when seen in its natural habitats it sometimes appears wild and rough. The Fell is good breeding stock and makes an ideal pony for trekking.

Description *Height* Up to 13·2 hands *Colours* Mostly entirely black, but some bays, browns or greys are seen *Head* This is small and well set on, with a broad forehead *Ears* Well formed and small *Neck* Strong, but not too heavy *Back, loins and quarters* A muscular body with strong and generous quarters. Powerful loins *Feet* Well shaped and tough on long and clean hocks *Tail* Well set and highly carried
Breed Society The Fell Pony Society

The Welsh pony

Accepted throughout the world as being among the most beautiful of all pony breeds, the Welsh also have superb qualities as children's riding ponies. Many, when thinking of the Welsh breeds, which are split into four sections, consider them as show ponies, seldom giving thought to the many types of other breeds which carry Welsh blood and which perform so well when jumping, eventing or hunting. The Welsh Stud Book caters for each of the separate sections which for many hundreds of years have lived and roamed on the Welsh mountains. They have developed a wonderful disposition and are intelligent, courageous and honest. The Sections shown in the Stud Book are quite distinctive and each has been given a detailed official description. No Welsh pony can be piebald or skewbald – all other colours are recognised.

These colts are typical Welsh mountain ponies.

The Welsh mountain pony (Section A)

A most beautiful pony whose height does not exceed 12 hands. It is sure-footed, sound and has the kindest of temperaments. Section A ponies have good movement and balance and are very safe in the hands of small children. They are natural jumpers and unequalled in the show ring. All Sections of the Stud Book are descended from the mountain pony and have these qualities.

Section A

The Welsh pony (Section B)

Larger than the pony in Section A, the Welsh pony stands at a height not above 13·2 hands. This breed is still used to carry a man shepherding and hunting in the hills of Wales. It is much in demand as a child's second pony, having all the qualities of the modern riding pony while retaining the type, character and hardiness of the native pony.

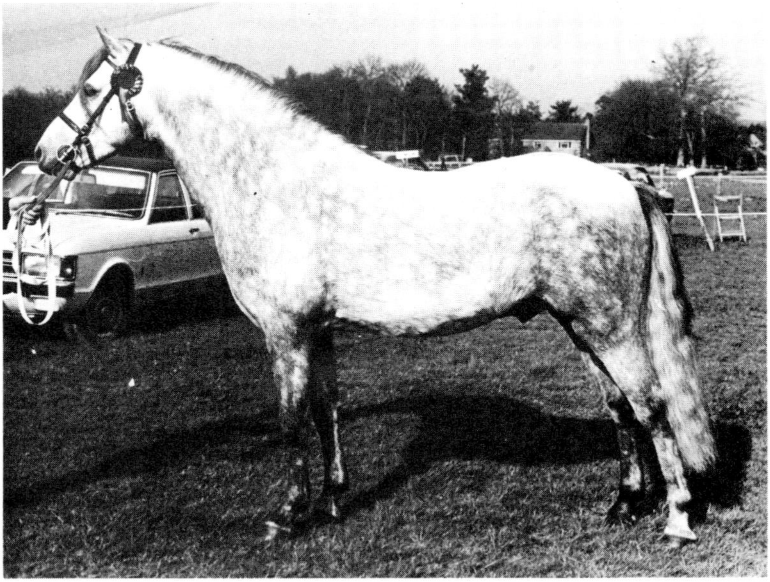

The Welsh pony or cob type (Section C)
The height must not exceed 13·2 hands. This is a very sure-footed pony who is capable of carrying either a full-grown man or a child. Used widely for hunting, trekking and in harness.

The Welsh cob (Section D)
A strong and active sort, useful for both riding and driving. Standing up to nearly 15·3 hands, the average Welsh cob is a little above the height of a pony. This particular breed is now one of the best of the smaller horses.
Breed Society (for all Sections) The Welsh Pony and Cob Society

Top left: Section B
Bottom left: Section C
Below: Section D

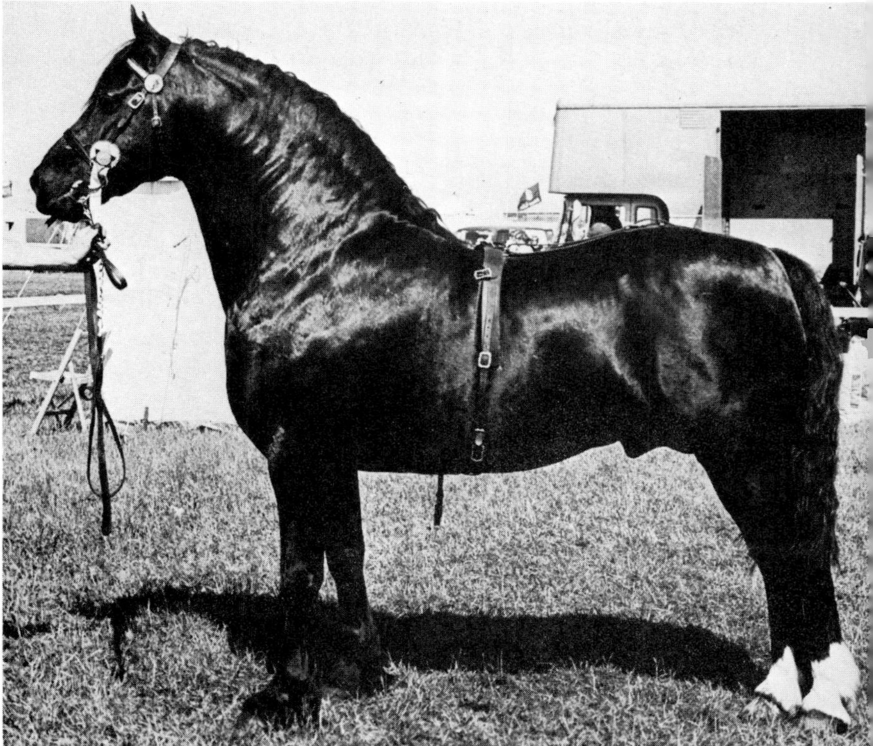

The Connemara pony

There is but one native breed of pony in Ireland, the Connemara. In the west of Ireland, near to the wild Atlantic Ocean, lies the district of Connemara, from which the breed has been named. This is a particularly rugged part of the country with a mixture of rocky ground, mountainous slopes, lakes and bogs – the ideal place to permit a hardy and intelligent pony to breed and thrive. Apart from a few of the more fertile valleys, the grazing is sparse and poor. And this has gone to make the Connemara a most hardy type of pony, well suited to life in the toughest of conditions.

As with so many mountain and moorland breeds, the Connemara has been crossed very successfully with Thoroughbred stock. This has produced a number of well-known internationally famous jumpers. But the pure-bred Connemara has a great variety of uses. It is valuable as a farm animal; it has a natural ability to jump; it is sure-footed and gentle in its approach, and yet it is bold and honest in its use in all forms of equestrian sport.

Standing just under 14 hands, the Connemara shows up well when judged alongside British native bred ponies.

Description (taken from the Stud Book) *Colour* Grey, black, bay, brown, dun, with occasional roans and chestnuts *Head* Well balanced head and neck *Body* Compact, deep, standing on short legs *Bone* Clean, hard, flat, measuring 7 to 8 inches (18 to 20 cm) below the knee *Action* Free, easy and true movement
Breed Society The Connemara Pony Society

The Dartmoor pony

The Dartmoor pony has from earliest times lived and roamed in a rugged part of south-west England. The area, swept in the winter months by high winds and severe gales, offers little in the way of feeding. Protection from the climate is found in and around the high tors and well-wooded lower slopes, but the moor is rock

strewn and only a very hardy and sure-footed pony would have survived. The Dartmoor is a great favourite as a children's riding pony, and is excellent foundation stock for the breeding of larger ponies. Standing at a maximum height of 12·2 hands, the Dartmoor offers practically everything one could look for in a pony – it is good looking, honest and gentle. With its hardy background and nature it makes an ideal pony to live out at grass.

Description *Height* Not exceeding 12·2 hands *Colours* Bay, black or brown preferred, but no colour bar except skewbald and piebald *Head* Small and breedy and well set *Ears* Small and alert *Neck* Not too long or too short. It should be strong, but not heavy *Back, loins and quarters* Strong and covered with muscle *Feet* Tough and well-shaped *Tail* Set high and quite full
Breed Society The Dartmoor Pony Society

The New Forest pony

The New Forest, which is in Hampshire, has many square miles of woodland, heath and marshy bogs. Today there are few parts which can be called true forest, and many of the native ponies, who have lived in the district since earliest times, run loose and live near to the roads which take thousands of holiday-makers in their cars towards the south-coast resorts and holiday centres in the south-west.

New Forest ponies are popular throughout the world, especially in Europe, and thrive in a variety of conditions. When cross-bred they produce excellent small hunters and make one of the best-tempered, kindly and gentle of riding ponies.

Standing between 12·2 hands and 14·2 hands, New Forest ponies, which can be any colour except piebald or skewbald, are up to any of the larger native breeds. For many years they were used extensively for general work on farms and small-holdings. They were also in demand as pack ponies, carrying quite heavy loads over long distances. With the introduction of blood from other breeds – both Arab and Thoroughbred – they are recognised as one of the best all-round ponies in the world.

Description *Height* Varies from 12 hands to 14·2 hands *Colours* Any colour except piebald and skewbald *Head* Well set on *Back, loins and quarters* Short with good strong loins and quarters.
Breed Society New Forest Pony Breeding and Cattle Society

New Forest pony

The Exmoor pony

On the wild and lonely moors, part of which are in Devon and part in Somerset, lives the oldest of the native pony breeds – the Exmoor. This is a sturdy, agile pony, though there are today few places on the moors where the pure-bred ponies live.

Like the Dartmoor, the Exmoor makes an excellent riding pony for children in spite of its small size. The true-bred Exmoor does not make more than 12·2 hands, though some of the stallions are found at 12·3 hands. Those that still live on the moors find little sustenance in the moorland grass – yet they thrive there, just as they have done since earliest times.

The Exmoor also makes a most useful hunter; it is safe-footed and highly intelligent. It is also most adaptable when put across severe courses in cross-country and other events.

Description *Height* Up to 12·3 hands for stallions; to 12·2 hands for mares *Colours* Bay, brown or dun, but no white markings anywhere. The muzzle and flanks are mealy *Head* Rather long with a

deep-set jaw *Ears* Short and thick with a mealy colour inside *Neck* Arched *Back, loins and quarters* The back is strong, and the chest is deep and wide *Feet* Neat and firm on short and clean legs
Breed Society The Exmoor Pony Society

Exmoor pony

The Shetland pony

The Shetland is the smallest of the British native ponies. It has been proved that it has maintained its small stature in its native Shetland Islands for over 2000 years. The extreme hardiness of the Shetland has enabled it to thrive under very adverse grazing and weather conditions, but it will enjoy life in any climate. If pure bred it will not become over-height. Shetlands, if they are Registered, must not stand above 40 inches (1·01 metres) at three years and under, and not more than 42 inches (1·06 metres) at four years and over.

Ideally, Shetland ponies thrive best on a large run of rough grazing, but, under proper management and conditions, they can well be kept in small fields and paddocks. Fresh water must always be available and hay is invariably essential to supplement the grass during winter months for all ponies.

Description *Colours* Any colour known in horses *Head* Small with a wide forehead. The muzzle must be broad *Ears* Neat and small and well-placed *Neck* Long, well arched and ending in a well defined wither *Back, loins and quarters* The body and loins must be strong and muscular, the quarters broad and long *Feet* Round, open and very hard *Tail* Long and straight and set high
Breed Society The Shetland Pony Stud Book Society

Douglas Bunn's magnificent Heavyweight Hunter, Selsey Bill, 16.3 hands and seven years of age. He has won many first prizes and Championships at major shows throughout the British Isles.

What are the breeds of horses?

The space available permits us to deal only briefly with horse breeds and breeding. We will look at the Arab and Thoroughbred, and would advise those who wish to know more about this vast subject to consult some of the many specialist books available.

Whether our intention is to buy a horse solely for hacking or hunting, or whether the horse we are looking for is to be used for showing, we are set with the problem we will face when seeking a horse for jumping – we have to find him! There is always a number of good quality horses for sale. And some not so good! Our difficulty comes in making a final decision, and making the right choice of breed or type.

The Arab

The Arab has had the greatest influence of all on the world's horse population. In practically every type, from the Thoroughbred to the heavy working horses, from show ponies to show hunters, we find strains of Arab blood. The Arab is a most beautiful animal, as the picture on page 18 shows. It can be traced back for more than 5000 years.

Standing usually between14·0 hands and 15·3 hands the Arab is not a big horse. It is renowned for its soundness, staying power and ability to carry weights which seem out of proportion to its size. It lives well in most climates, from desert wastes to the more lush grasslands of the northern and southern hemispheres.

Pure-bred Arabs are registered in the various stud books which are kept by the Arab Horse societies.

Captain Elwyn Hartley Edwards has written: 'All horses in competitive sport derive from the Arab to some extent and as a pure-bred he is supreme in the long distance endurance rides, though in his pure form he plays hardly any part in show-jumping or three-day events. Arab blood, outside strictly Thoroughbred breeding, continues to play a vital part in the development and upgrading of other breeds.' (*The Complete Book of the Horse* published by Ward Lock, London)

The *Anglo-Arab*, now popular in showing classes, show-jumping, eventing and other fields of equestrian sport, is the result of the cross of Arab and Thoroughbred. This, to many people, is the perfect saddle horse. Bigger than the pure-bred Arab, it stands between 15 hands and 16·3 hands.

The Thoroughbred

The modern Thoroughbred traces its ancestry back to three Arabian stallions which were brought to England during the latter part of the seventeenth century and the early part of the eighteenth century. These were the Byerley Turk, the Darley Arabian and the Godolphin Arabian.

Today, the Thoroughbred will still show traces of his Arabian beginnings and the breed has had enormous influence on many breeds throughout the world. Many show ponies are a cross of their native breed with part Arab or Thoroughbred.

With its long, easy action, and great turn of speed, the Thoroughbred is today principally found in the world of horse racing. Usually standing between 15·3 hands and 17 hands, it makes an excellent riding horse, with superb conformation.

A good all-round horse suitable for all types of equestrian activities. The horse and rider, both well turned-out, are ready to compete in a Riding class.

Right: A British Spotted pony, which is similar to the Appaloosa.

Though frequently excitable and difficult to manage in show-jumping and dressage competitions, the Thoroughbred is perhaps the ideal cross, often being mated with half-bred mares or with Arab or Anglo-Arab crosses.

Other horses

Not all horses are bred from Arab or Thoroughbred stock. The ancestors of many successful show jumpers and eventers can not be traced. Perhaps all too frequently breeding and cross-breeding is haphazard. In many cases owners may know something about the sire of their horse, but will look blank when asked about the dam. This does not necessarily take away from them the confidence and pleasure they get from owning a horse. Some are lucky enough to own a pure-bred, others would not change their part-bred for anything in the world.

Among some of the well-known breeds from the world of horses are: Andalusian (Spain); Ardennais (France and parts of Western Europe); Appaloosa (United States); Breton (France); Cleveland Bay (Great Britain); Haflinger (Austria); Hanoverian (Germany); Holstein (Germany); Irish Draught (Ireland); Lipizzaner (Austria); Morgan (United States); Pahlavan (Iran); Palomino (United States); Percheron (France); Quarter Horse (United States); Shire (Great Britain); Waler (Australia).

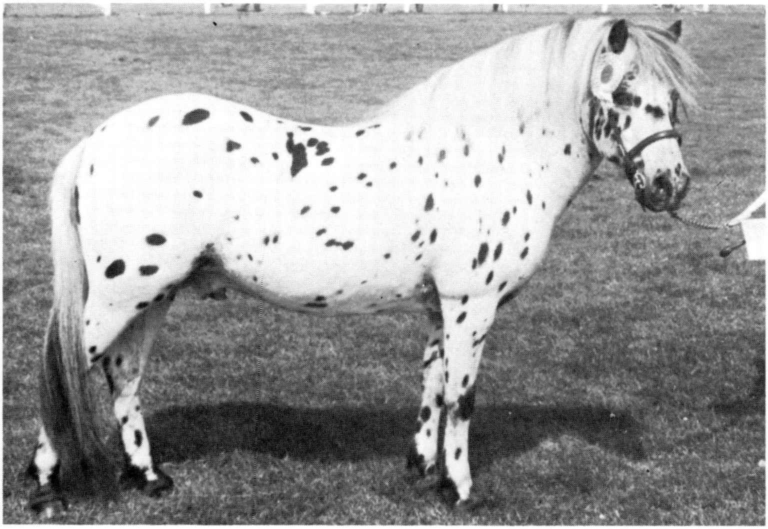

By what colours are horses and ponies known?

As a general rule the following show the recognised colourings:

Black A black body with black mane and tail.

Brown Dark brown colouring overall, with brown mane and tail.

Bay Brown body with black mane and tail and black points, i.e., the muzzle, tips of ears and the lower part of the limbs.

Chestnut A reddish-brown body with mane and tail of similar colouring. Variations of the chestnut are the 'light chesnut', 'dark chestnut' and 'liver chestnut'.

Dun Body varying from a cream to a shade of yellow. Usually found with a black mane, tail and points, and with a black line running along the back.

Grey A coat which has a mixture of grey and black hairs. There are several varieties according to age, season and type – but all are known as 'grey'. A light grey would describe a very white-looking horse or pony.

Piebald A horse or pony with large irregular patches of black and white on the body and black and white hairs in the mane and tail.

Skewbald A horse or pony with large irregular patches of white and any other colour except black.

Roan A difficult colour to describe. Usually a roan appears to be a mixture of chestnut, bay or black with a light grey fleck throughout the coat. There are three types – 'strawberry', 'bay' and 'blue'.

What are the names given to the different markings?

Blaze A broad white mark down the face. This usually spreads over the bones of the nose.

Snip A white mark between the nostrils.

Star A white mark on the forehead.

Stripe A narrow white mark down the face.

White face Where the colour includes the eyes, nose, part of the muzzle and the forehead.

Wall eye Where there is a lack of pigment in the iris. This gives a white or a bluish-white appearance.

blaze **star** **stripe** **white face**

Stocking A white leg which reaches up as far as the knee or hock.

Sock Involves the fetlock and part of the region near to the cannon.

White fetlock, white coronet or white pastern Describes a particular part of a leg.

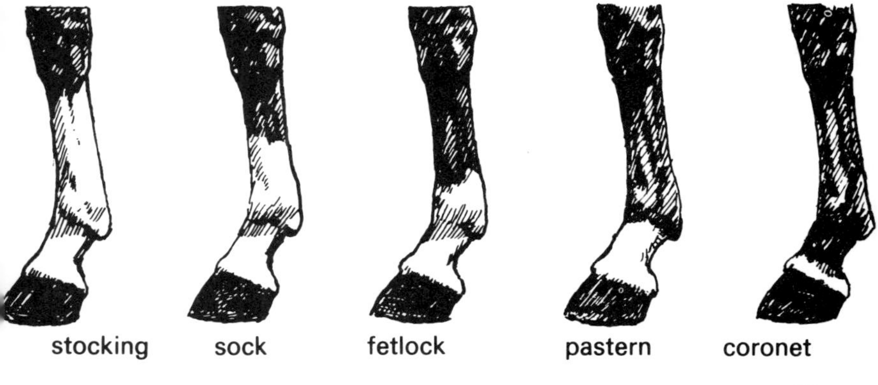

stocking **sock** **fetlock** **pastern** **coronet**

Looking after a horse or pony

What is a stable-kept pony?

Unlike the grass-kept pony, who will be living out throughout the year, the stable-kept animal is kept in though preferably allowed some grazing each day.

The constant attention to the cleanliness of the stable and its surrounds are only part of the work a stable-kept pony demands. He requires feeding at regular times, plenty of fresh water, a thorough grooming each day, a planned work programme, daily 'mucking out' and a clean and dry bed each night.

One advantage a stable-kept pony has over a grass-kept pony is that he will always be to hand when you decide to ride, exercise or school. He will never present the problem of first having to be caught!

What is a grass-kept pony?

This expression means, in simple terms, that the pony is kept at grass all the time and is not brought in to a stable at night, or when the weather becomes wet or cold.

There are a great number of advantages in having a grass-kept pony, especially a pony who will come to hand when called! Ponies living in this way enjoy a more natural environment and will feed from grass which is their natural food. They will also be able to eat as and when they choose and to exercise themselves at will.

But there are some disadvantages. Ponies at grass are not always easy to catch, and fields and paddocks are not easily found! Each day it is necessary for a grass-kept pony to be caught and tied up to a gate, post or tree, since regular examination for injuries and grooming must be carried out. His feet must be picked out and checked for soundness, and at the same time the condition of the shoes must be noted.

In the book *Keeping a Pony at Grass* (published by the British Horse Society) the needs of a pony kept at grass are simply and clearly explained. Among the rules for the grass-kept pony are:

1 Make certain there is always fresh and clean water available.
2 Ensure there is a shelter in the field or paddock.
3 Look the pony over each day.
4 Make a regular inspection of all fences and gates.
5 Clean away and burn all dangerous weeds, etc.
6 Visit the farrier as and when required.
7 See the pony supplements its feed by having hay each day during late autumn and throughout the winter months.
8 If possible, let the pony enjoy a change of grazing.
9 Try to give a pony companionship by having more than one pony in the field.

How much land is required for grazing?

It is not possible to state exactly the area of land that is required, since this depends very largely on the type of land available, the nature of the soil, the drainage and the location. A minimum is usually quoted as 2·5 hectares (one acre) for a small pony, but more than this where a single pony is being kept. The reasons for this are twofold: one, that part of any land must be laid up to enable the grazing to be rested and properly 'dressed' and, two, to ensure the area is not over-grazed. Ponies will only eat the grasses that they enjoy. They would go without rather than eat the rank, tufty type of grass that will grow around their droppings.

The removal of droppings by shovel and wheelbarrow is one of the best methods of keeping the grazing in good shape. This is something that must be done regularly, preferably every few days.

An ideal arrangement is when you can have other animals grazing over the land that is being rested. Cattle will enjoy the longer, rough grass that ponies have refused. In this way the land can be kept fresher and more evenly-grazed.

Can the condition of land be improved?

When one talks of the condition of land one must always think of the problem of drainage. On much of land which has a sandy or chalky soil this is not such a major problem. But when the grazing land is on clay good drainage is essential for good pasture.

If the land is really poor it is better to have it ploughed up and completely re-seeded. The mixture of seed will be important and advice should be taken from local farmers or from the seedsman. The selection of the best seed varies according to the soil, but it should include a mixture of grasses and clover with some of the herbs ponies enjoy.

The addition of lime and phosphates to the soil will also help towards improving the grazing, as will the occasional use of a harrow and roller.

The improvement of land demands a certain scientific knowledge of the problems involved. As with many of the difficulties faced when owning or caring for horses and ponies, always talk to those with experience and seek the advice of specialists.

Which trees and hedge plants are dangerous to ponies?
Yew and laburnum are the most dangerous trees and even the dead and half-dead branches when eaten can quickly poison a pony. Oaks are also to be avoided, since acorns eaten in excess can cause death. One must also do everything to keep ponies from laurel, acacia or rhododendron hedges.

Most poisonous plants will only affect the pony's health when eaten to excess. But it is far better to avoid the problem which might arise by removing from the fields and hedgerows all plants, hedge plants and trees which are dangerous.

Never take a chance with a pony's health – especially if trouble can be prevented by continual and thorough inspection.

Make regular checks in the hedgerows around the paddock or field. Look at more than the condition of the post-and-rail fencing or wire, though this too is important. It can happen that trees and hedge plants, which may be growing out of the reach of ponies in a field, will produce a shoot or extend a branch making it all too easy for a pony to reach.

Never feel sure all is safe until you get into a routine of regular inspection.

Which plants are dangerous to ponies?
Some of the most dangerous plants are ragwort, hemlock, foxglove, henbane, horsetail, ground ivy, privet. Where these appear on the land it is best if they are dug up, taken from the field, and put on a fire. It is not a good idea to pull the tops off – it is far better to get rid of the roots as well!

Fields need regular and thorough inspection especially between spring and early autumn.

What is the best form of fencing?

A post and rail fence is perhaps the best of all artificial types of fencing. This should be erected to a height which will prevent a horse or pony from jumping out of the field. Among alternatives are electric fences (these are not recommended, except when reducing the area being used for grazing) and the fencing which uses wire.

When wire is used there is a danger in this becoming broken and rusty. The upright posts to which the wires are attached can also become loose in the ground – sometimes because horses and ponies will use them to rub up against.

Barbed wire as a means of fencing is to be avoided.

The most natural fence is that formed by hedges and banks. Again, these require frequent attention to see that gaps are not appearing.

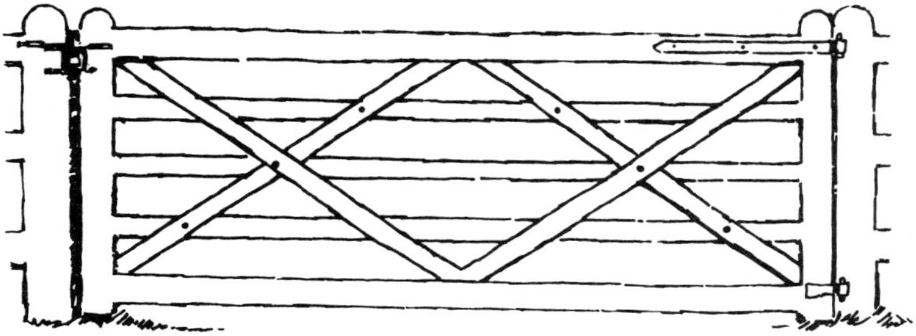

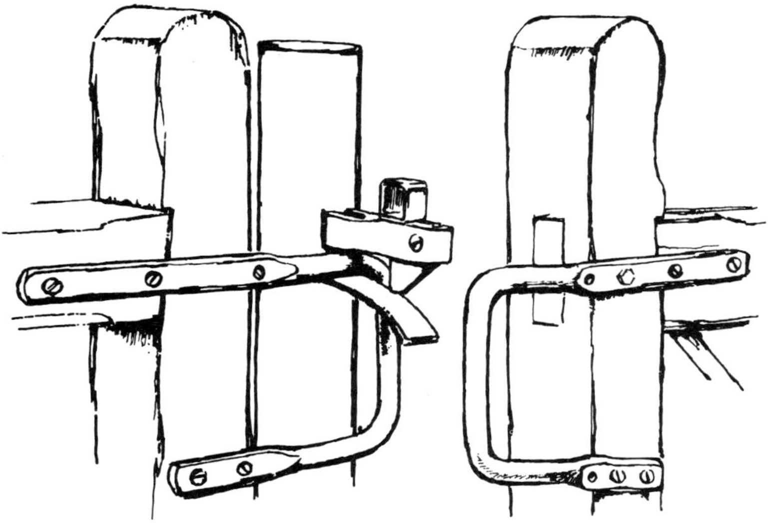

What is the best type of gate?

A gate to a field or paddock must have two qualities: it must be strong and easy to open, yet it must be simple to close and secure. A gate should also be wide enough to permit a horse-box or tractor to get in and out of the field.

Gates made from wood or from metal should be hung on strong upright posts. Be sure the fastening is such that the gate is secure when shut.

If you feel it necessary to lock a gate a chain with a padlock is perhaps the best method. Making gates too secure can be quite a nuisance, especially when they may require opening in a hurry or in the case of an emergency.

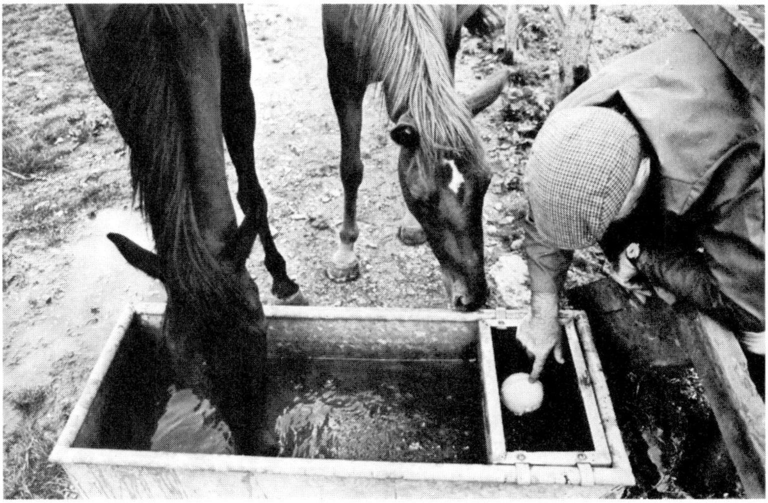

The drinking trough is being checked. When the ball-cock is gently pressed, the flow of fresh water can be seen to be refilling the trough freely.

Is running water essential?

The best possible supply of water in a field used for grazing is a running stream or pond, but not a pond that is silted or stagnant. Should neither of these be available the best alternative is to have water brought to the field through pipes.

This will mean having a trough, similar to the one illustrated. As ponies drink the level of water lowers and the ball-cock (which regulates the fresh water coming into the trough) opens, allowing water to flow through to re-fill the trough.

If a trough is in use a regular inspection is necessary to see that it is flowing freely and not flooding. The trough must be thoroughly cleaned out and scrubbed each month.

Static water, that is water kept in an old bath or other container, can be dangerous to the health of a pony. Unless there is a regulator or ball-cock fitted to the supply it is far better to bring fresh water in buckets. These should be re-filled twice a day and must be place on level ground to avoid them being easily knocked over.

In winter months the troughs or buckets must be looked at quite frequently to see that ice has not formed which will prevent a pony from getting his essential drink.

Which form of shelter is best?

There are really two types of shelter, the natural protection which comes from trees and hedgerows and the man-made shelter which looks like an open-fronted stable. Both are essential to the well-being of horses and ponies which are grazed for long periods.

In summer months the horses and ponies will shelter to escape from flies and heat, and if they can do this inside a wooden shelter so much the better. In winter months this shelter will then give protection from winds and rain.

We picture the ideal type of shelter. It should be placed in the corner of a field, preferably with its back to the prevailing winds. Trees and stout hedges also give protection, but these are not always effective in winter months when the leaves have fallen and the hedges are not as thick as they are in summer.

Why cleanliness?

The most important rule to be observed by all who own or look after horses or ponies is to ensure cleanliness. Paddocks and fields must be attended to and, as far as stable-kept horses are concerned, cleanliness has to be ensured at all times both in the stable and around the stable area.

At regular periods the entire stable must be cleaned out and the floor and walls brushed and hosed. Then, when the floor is completely dry, the bedding can be put back. It is also important that the manger and other feeding utensils are cleaned each day.

The area surrounding a stable should be more than tidy! Do not allow any dirt or litter to lie about. Without a constant watch that all is clean and tidy there is a risk of disease.

Apart from a clean stable, clean food and water, and a clean and fresh bed, a horse must be kept clean by regular and thorough grooming.

The 'muck heap', too, must be looked at each week. See that this is well sited; neither too far from nor too near the stable. The heap should be removed as often as necessary.

What different materials can be used for bedding?

It is essential to do all you can to provide the best possible bed for your horse or pony. The aim is for a warm and dry bed, and this can always be provided when you regularly carry out the preparation and cleaning of the stable.

The 'mucking out' of a stable, or shelter, is perhaps the most important of all routine stable jobs. It must be done at least once a day and, where a horse or pony is stable-kept, it may have to be carried out each morning and evening.

The different materials which can be used for bedding include:

1 Straw
2 Bracken or peat
3 Wood chips or shavings
4 Sawdust.

Of these, straw is perhaps the most commonly used; the different types of straw and varying lengths to which it has been cut allow you to provide an ideal bed. When mucking out a straw bed a certain amount of the material will be taken away in the wheelbarrow. This should be stacked on the muck heap.

Bracken or peat are not really as suitable, though either can serve the purpose when other materials are not to hand.

Wood chips or wood shavings are used in many stables, sometimes by choice and sometimes when the vet has advised taking a horse which might have slight breathing difficulties off a straw bed.

Whatever material is used be sure to clean it daily. Bedding of straw, bracken, peat, sawdust or shavings can be dusty. Never fork too violently, and when cleaning out a stable and re-making a bed allow any dust to settle before putting your horse or pony back into the stable.

What are the rules of good feeding?

The most natural way for a horse or pony to feed is by grazing, though with the changing seasons and different climatic conditions, the goodness in grass will vary from very rich to extremely poor. Therefore, when a pony is asked to work, some supplementary feeding is necessary and the nature of such supplementary feeding depends (a) on the nature and extent of the work being asked for, and (b) on the pony's age, condition and temperament.

To a large extent you will have to judge what your horse or pony requires to keep him well-fed and fit. You will notice by his appearance whether or not his condition is falling off or whether he is putting on too much fat.

The questions which must be answered to determine the amount and type of feed are:

1 What is the nature and amount of work being given?
2 What is the age and size of the horse or pony?
3 What is the condition of the grazing?
4 What is the season? Is it springtime with its lush and sometimes too rich grass? Or is it winter with little grass and certainly no nourishment in what there is?

Here are some simple rules towards good feeding practices which have proved invaluable for horse and pony owners. These should be studied and used at all times.

If a pony is stabled or part-stabled:

Rule 1 Feed little and often.
Rule 2 Wherever possible some grazing should take place each day.
Rule 3 Each day give the horse or pony a bulk food, such as hay.
Rule 4 Feed at the same time each day.
Rule 5 Always feed good, clean forage.
Rule 6 Do not make any sudden changes to the type of feed. If a change is to be made introduce it gradually.
Rule 7 Never work a horse or pony immediately after a feed.
Rule 8 Water before feeding, but always keep fresh water available in the stable. Allow a horse or pony to drink as it will, whether or not it is having a big or short feed.
Rule 9 Feed according to the work done, but always abide by Rule 3.

How should hay be fed and how much is required?

Wherever possible hay should be given in haynets, suitably filled and hung on a strong fence or at the correct height in the stable. Nets must be fixed quite firmly, and high enough to prevent a pony catching a foot in it after the net is emptied and hanging loose. Except in very severe winter conditions, and when feeding ponies kept at grass, no hay should be spread on the ground. This can only result in most of it being left and wasted.

Three different sizes of haynets can be bought, the largest of which will hold between 4·5 and 6 kg (12 and 14 lb) of hay. A medium-sized net will hold between 3·5 and 4 kg (8 and 9 lb) of hay, and a small net (suitable only for the very smallest of ponies) up to 2 kg (4 lb).

Most ponies are given a medium-sized net, which will mean if being fed twice a day a pony will be taking about 8 kg (18 lb) during

a twenty-four hour period. If we think he will be given this amount each day throughout the winter months we know he will require 8 (the number of kg) × 7 (the number of days in a week) × 26 (the number of weeks in a half year). We now find that the pony will require 1456 kg in that period! And that is not giving him any hay during the other half of the year!!

The stable and equipment

Why were horses first stabled?

Anyone who has trudged across a muddy field in an effort to catch an unwilling horse or pony and then spent hours trying to make him look smart will know the answer to this question.

As soon as people started to take an interest in their own appearance, they also wanted their horses to look attractive, and developed a pride in the way in which they were turned out. They realised however that this was more difficult with an animal that was allowed to roam about all the year round.

A stable was the obvious answer because it not only provided protection in bad weather, it also ensured that the animal was always on hand when needed. By the careful control of food and exercise, a stabled horse could also be kept in really hard condition and ready for any strenuous work its owner might require it to do.

Loose boxes give freedom for a horse to look out.

What is a loose box and why is it the best form of stabling?

Although many horses and ponies are kept quite happily in stalls, loose boxes allow greater freedom, enabling them to lie down and rest more easily. They can roll at will, and get a certain amount of exercise by walking round the box.

The loose box must have good headroom, be reasonably large, and be free from any sharp objects which could cause injury.

Doors should be of the type which open in two parts enabling the upper portion to be hooked back so that the animal can look out. Special safety latches are necessary to prevent him from opening the doors, which must also be wide enough to prevent a horse being led from the stable from brushing against a door post and damaging not only itself but also the saddlery. All light fittings and switches should be of the safety variety.

Mangers need to be fixed securely to the wall and should be deep enough to prevent a horse from throwing out its food, but high enough to prevent it from becoming cast underneath.

Most owners use hay nets because they are easy to fill and cause less mess, but they should always be tied up at a height to give a natural feeding position, and prevent seeds and dust from getting into the horse's eyes.

All stabled animals need plenty of fresh water, and the water buckets should be kept full.

What is the best form of stable flooring?

Various forms of flooring are used in stables, but it is essential to ensure that whatever material is used is of the non-slip variety. It should also be impervious to moisture, long wearing, and reasonably warm and comfortable for a horse lying down.

Although concrete is the material in most frequent use, it is not entirely satisfactory, although it has the benefit in most countries of being relatively cheap and easy to obtain. If concrete is used, the surface must always be roughened to enable a horse or pony to get a grip, and not to slip when getting up and down, otherwise injury can occur.

Stable bricks are the best solution, but they are expensive and unfortunately no longer in plentiful supply.

In order to ensure good drainage and prevent the bedding from becoming too wet, the stable floor should be made to slope slightly. Shallow channel-drains either just inside or just outside the stable doorway usually provide the most efficient type of runaway, and are easy to keep clean. They can be connected either to a soak-away or to the main drain in the stable yard.

Covered drains inside the stables are less efficient because they can become clogged by the bedding, and are consequently more difficult to maintain.

Why is ventilation so important?

Horses and ponies need plenty of fresh air if they are to keep really fit and free from coughs and colds. Animals kept in stables which are stuffy and badly ventilated because their owners have the mistaken idea that they are providing warmth, are usually those who easily become victims of seasonal ailments.

Horses don't like draughts, and everything should be done to block up cracks and badly fitting window frames. If the stable faces south, and the bottom portion of the door is high enough to exclude draughts, it is as well to leave the top of the stable door open day and night, all the year round.

All stables should have a window, not only to provide natural light, but also as a means of additional ventilation. The best type is the kind which opens inwards, so that fresh air is directed upwards towards the stable roof, and not directly on to the animal's back.

Warmth in cold weather should be provided by rugs, and an additional blanket in winter, particularly if the horse or pony is fully clipped.

What is the best form of bedding?

Some form of suitable bedding is necessary in any stall or stable, not only to prevent a horse's feet from becoming jarred from standing for long hours on a hard floor, but also to encourage it to stale freely, and to provide a comfortable bed when it lies down to rest.

Straw is usually looked upon as being the best bedding material, but owing to rising costs wood shavings, sawdust and peat are also being used. Good quality shavings are certainly better than poor quality and dusty straw.

A stable barrow, shovel, broom, stable fork with blunt points, a four-pronged fork and a dung skip will be needed for mucking out a stable containing straw bedding.

If shavings, sawdust or peat are used, a long handled wire rake and a pair of rubber gloves will also be required. It is important for the droppings to be removed frequently during the day to prevent them from being trodden into the bedding. The rubber gloves are very handy for this purpose. Every morning all the droppings and very wet bedding should be removed, and the surface raked level.

In the evening a clean layer should be spread over the floor of the box, and the underneath layer can be used to bank up the sides of the stable as an added protection when the horse lies down.

Every few weeks, according to the size of the horse or pony and the size of the stable, all the wet and soiled material should be dug out and replaced with fresh bedding.

Specially treated shredded paper is a relatively new form of bedding which has been tried quite successfully in some stables, and the mucking out process is very much the same as for wood shavings.

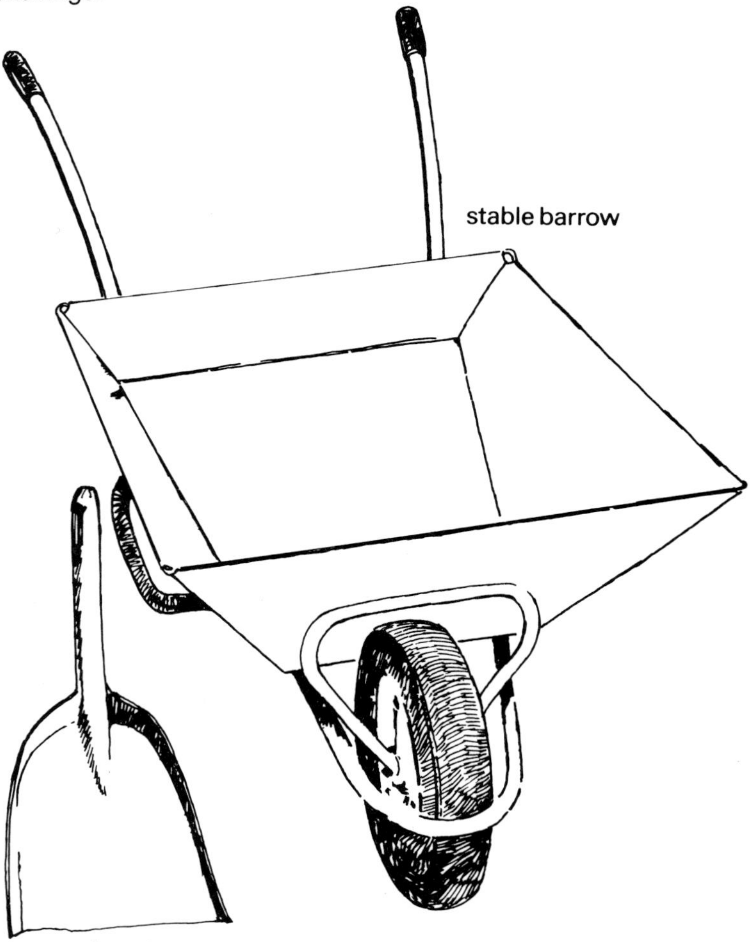

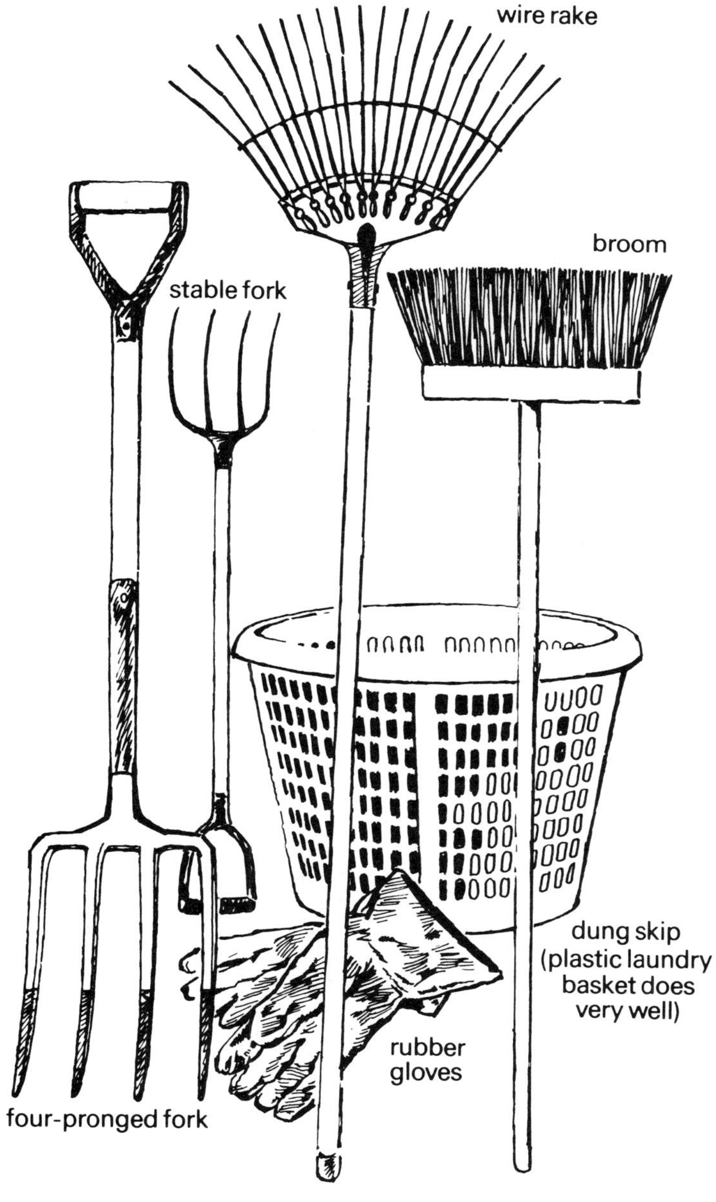
wire rake
broom
stable fork
dung skip
(plastic laundry
basket does
very well)
rubber
gloves
four-pronged fork

What is a normal stable routine?

The manner in which the various stable duties can be fitted into the work of the day must of course depend on whether there is someone looking after the horse full time, and the purpose for which it is being used.

Whatever decision is finally made regarding the daily timetable, it is important to remember that whereas horses and ponies get bored if they are exercised over the same route every day, they nevertheless do like to stick to a regular stable routine as far as is possible.

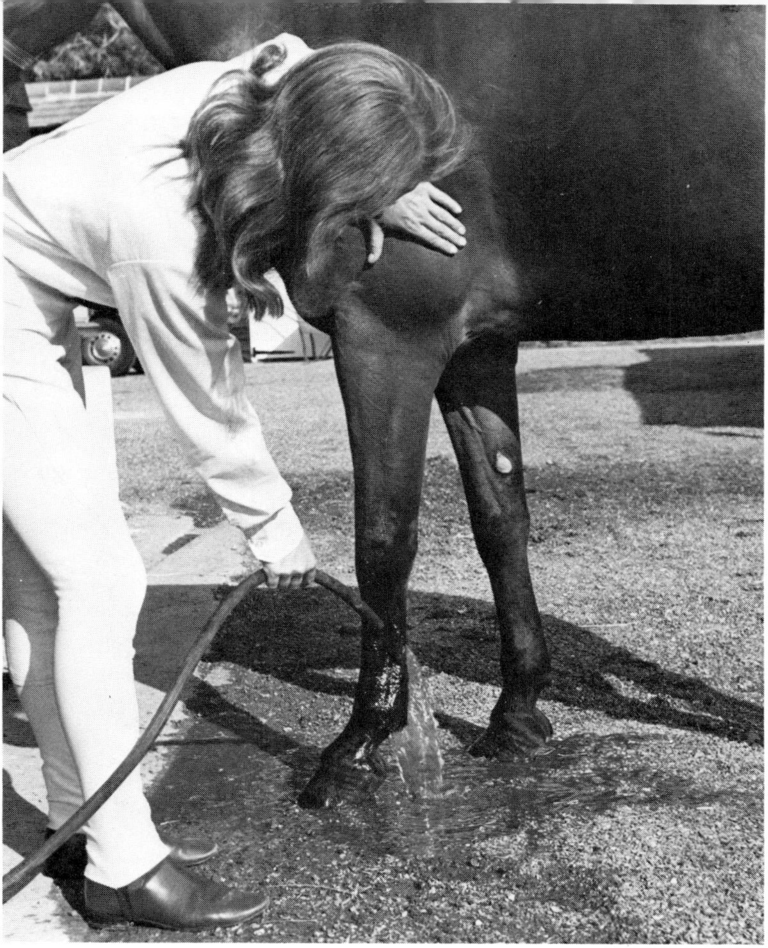

A horse with tendon trouble will benefit from having his legs hosed down after exercise on hard ground.

Horses and ponies, unlike their owners, always like an early start to the day, and if you are planning four feeds in the course of the day, it is as well to begin stables at about 6.30 a.m.

After tying him up with a headcollar, take a good look round to make sure your horse has not suffered any injury during the night. Then adjust the rugs, and make sure the water buckets are full.

A small net of hay will give him something to nibble, and keep him occupied while you muck out, and pick out his feet. The rugs should again be checked and he will then be ready for his first feed of the day at 7.30 a.m.

You must leave at least an hour between feed time and exercise, and this will give you time for your own breakfast and to check on the day's requirements.

At 9.0 a.m. you can remove his rugs, give him a quick brush over to remove any bits of bedding, and then tack him up for the morning's exercise. On returning to the stable take off his saddle and bridle, make sure he still has enough water, and allow him to stale. If you have been careful to walk the last part of the ride your horse should not be too hot, but if he is put on a sweat sheet and cover it with a light blanket and surcingle (see pages 92-7).

Now it's your turn for exercise. Tie him up and get to work to give him a thorough grooming while he is still warm. When you are satisfied with the results, and he begins to look ten times the horse he was when you started, put on his day rugs, refill the water bucket, let him loose and give him his second feed of the day. While he is eating this put up a full net of the best hay you can find and leave him to enjoy the next few hours to himself. There will be plenty of jobs for you to do around the stable and yard, and checking the state of the feed room.

At 4 p.m., if you really want to spoil your horse, take him in a tit-bit and make a fuss of him before tying him up and removing all the droppings and any damp bedding. Then pick out his feet into a dung skip, and bed down. Replace his day rug with the night rug, and a blanket if it's a cold winter night, refill the water buckets, untie him and remove his headcollar.

By 4.30 p.m. he will be ready for his third feed, and you should be ready for a tack cleaning session.

About 7.0 p.m. remove any droppings, refill his water buckets, tie up a full net of hay and give him his fourth and last feed.

Most important Last thing at night before you go to bed, slip quietly into the stables and make sure he is all right. It will be some hours before morning stables, and a last look round is always wise.

What is the ideal stable plan?

When planning a stable layout, the placing of various important areas must be considered – i.e., hay and straw barns, muck-heaps, fodder rooms and tack rooms.

Stables should preferably be within sight of the house so that the horses or ponies can be seen; essential extras like a fodder room and tack room can be incorporated to form windbreaks at either end of the stables.

Some form of hay and straw barns will also be needed but these should be placed to avoid any risk of fire. If large quantities of hay and straw are required the barns should be away from the main stable block.

Muck-heaps need to be placed somewhere handy to the stables, and an easy and firm approach for the muck lorry is essential.

Tack rooms need to be dry and secure, and apart from wall racks for the saddles and bridles, it is also important to have good storage for spare rugs, bandages, less frequently used tack, cleaning materials and if possible a sink with hot and cold running water. A table and saddle horse are also very useful.

Fodder rooms need to be within easy reach of the stables and they must be dry and vermin-proof. If you do get vermin, don't use rat poison which is highly dangerous to other animals and children. Ask for expert advice or better still keep a good stable cat. All foodstuff should be kept in vermin-proof bins, and plastic dustbins are excellent for this purpose.

A stable plan which shows a most practical and workable layout.

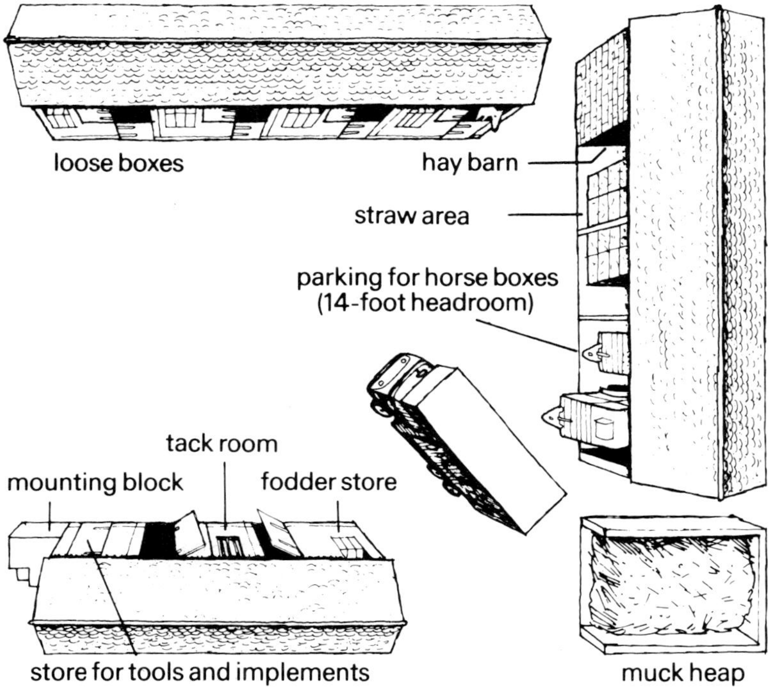

The care of the horse

Why is grooming important?

In his natural environment a horse would be able to roll and exercise at will, but if he is denied this freedom, his skin and feet can suffer unless he gets a thorough daily grooming. It should be remembered that the skin is as vital an organ to a horse's health as either his lungs or his heart.

Grooming has five main objectives: to promote health; to maintain condition; to prevent disease; to ensure cleanliness; and to improve appearance.

The grooming kit is consequently an essential part of every horse owner's equipment. A hoof pick is necessary for cleaning out the feet; a dandy brush will be needed for removing dirt and caked mud; the body brush will remove dust and scurf from the coat; and the steel curry comb will help keep the brush clean. A rubber curry comb is sometimes used along with the dandy brush to remove mud from the coat, particularly when a horse or pony has been out in the field. The water brush is important because when dampened it can lay the mane and tail, and clean the feet. A stable sponge will be necessary for cleaning the muzzle, eyes and dock, and a wisp will massage and promote the circulation. A stable rubber will provide a final polish.

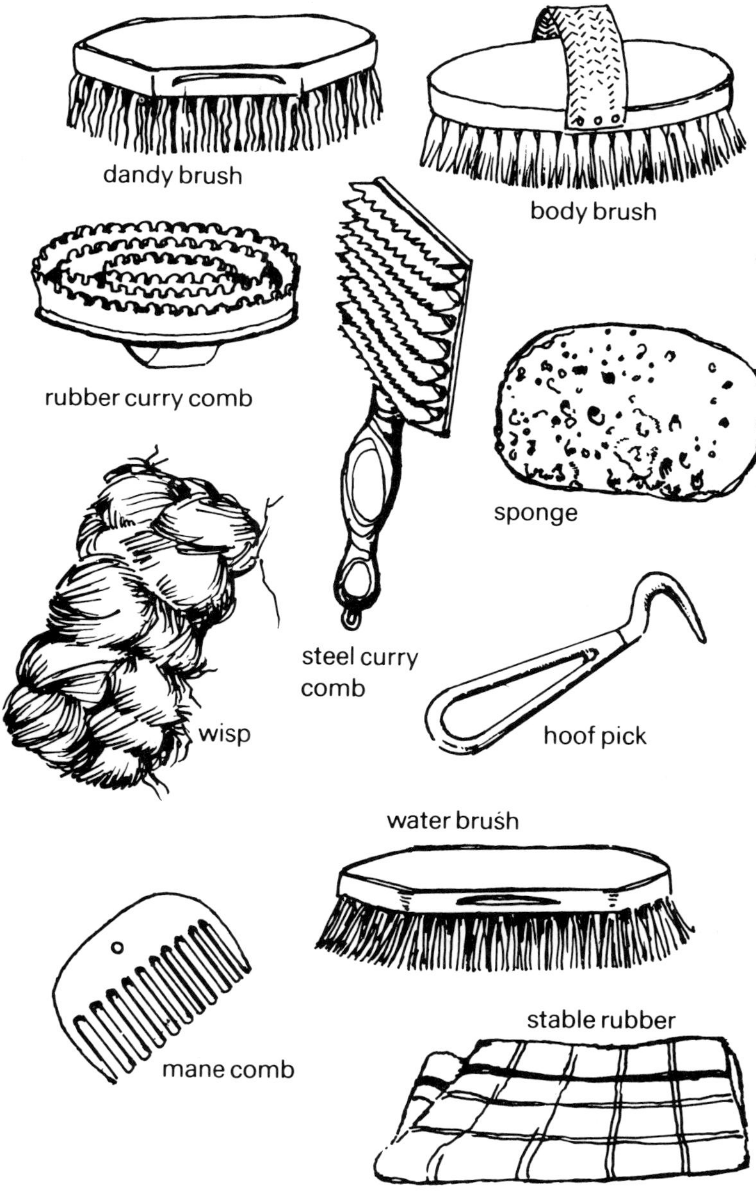
dandy brush
body brush
rubber curry comb
steel curry comb
sponge
wisp
hoof pick
water brush
mane comb
stable rubber

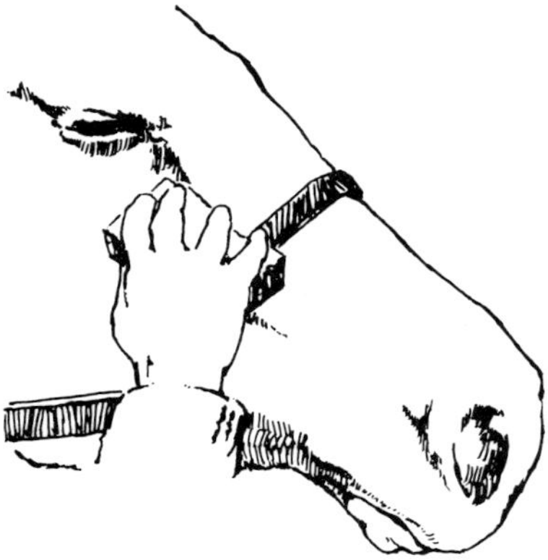

What is the importance of exercise?

A horse or pony in constant use needs sufficient exercise to keep him healthy and fit without causing him any undue exertion and loss of condition. If a horse is to maintain condition, exercise is essential.

When an animal is fat and has too big a belly, and his muscles are slack so that he is unable to do any fast work without sweating and showing signs of distress, he is said to be in 'soft' condition. He is looked upon as being in 'hard' condition when he is free of superfluous fat, and his muscles and tendons can withstand sustained effort without damage or distress.

It is important to know when your horse is really fit. The fat, round horse or pony at grass is likely to have soft and flabby muscles including those of his heart and lungs. His large belly will also occupy some of the space needed for his lungs to expand properly.

Once he is fit, however, the muscles of his limbs will be able to stand up to the strain of fast work without becoming tired, or worse still, breaking down. The muscles of his heart will be equal to the demands placed upon them, and those of his chest will help him to breathe fully and easily. The fat belly will have disappeared so that it will no longer be pressing on the chest to interfere with breathing, and the lungs will have greater space in which to work properly.

Two essentials are necessary to convert an animal from the soft to hard condition: sufficient food of the right kind, and the correct amount of the right work.

Slow steady exercise is important. Fast trotting and galloping will never get a horse or pony fit: indeed it will be more likely to do harm.

Once the animal is fit he will need regular exercise in order to keep him in 'hard' condition.

How would you feed a stabled horse or pony?

Grazing is of course the natural system of feeding, and grass is the horse's natural food. A horse in its natural environment will eat a little at a time throughout the day and night, and because of this it has a remarkably small stomach. That is why 'little and often' is the rule to remember when feeding a stabled horse or pony. The whole art of feeding properly is this adjustment so that the 'artificial' system of feeding comes as near as possible to the 'natural'.
Always remember these basic rules:

1 Whenever it is practical to do so feed little and often.

2 Feed plenty of bulk food such as hay, so that the digestive organs have some food in them all the time.

3 Feed according to the work the horse is doing, particularly as far as concentrated foods like oats are concerned. If the horse or pony is doing a lot of work the amount of concentrates can be increased, but always be very careful when feeding oats to a pony. If the amount of work is reduced, feed less concentrates, but remember to compensate by feeding more bulk food like hay.

4 Always water before feeding otherwise the undigested food will be washed out of the stomach and all the goodness lost. It is better to keep fresh water in the stable all the time, and it won't matter then if the horse takes a short drink during or after its meal.

5 Try and feed something succulent every day to compensate for the loss of grass. Allowing a horse to graze for a few minutes can be very beneficial.

6 Because the stomach lies alongside the chest it can press on the lungs when full and restrict the breathing. For this reason a horse should never be exercised until at least an hour after it has finished its meal.

7 Never make any sudden change in diet. Any adjustment in the type of food or in the feeding routine should be made gradually over a number of days.

8 Only feed clean good-quality food. Feeding musty and dusty food will only lead to trouble and expensive vet's bills.

9 Keep to regular hours of feeding, not only because it is better for the horse's digestive system, but also because a horse looks forward to its food, and a disappointed horse will usually end up with a disappointed rider.

How would you clip and trim a horse or pony?

There are six main reasons for clipping a horse.

1 To enable it to do fast work without becoming unduly distressed.

2 To keep its condition by preventing undue sweating.

3 To enable grooming to be carried out more easily.

4 To help a horse to dry off more easily and quickly after fast work or exercise.

5 To allow a horse to work faster and better for longer.

6 To prevent disease.

A change in the horse's appearance usually occurs about September, when the coat appears to become dull and rough. The winter coat starts to grow, but it must be allowed time to become fully established before you think about giving your horse the first clip of the winter.

The first clip usually takes place about October, and, depending on the horse, the second clip should not be made after the beginning of January.

There are various types of clip:

The full clip In this clip the whole of the coat is removed.

The hunter clip Also a major clip, in that all the hair is removed, with exception that hair is left on the legs as far as the elbows and thighs, and a saddle patch is left on the back. The coat is left on the legs as a protection against cold, injury from thorns, mud, and cracked heels. The saddle patch is left to give protection against a sore or scalded back.

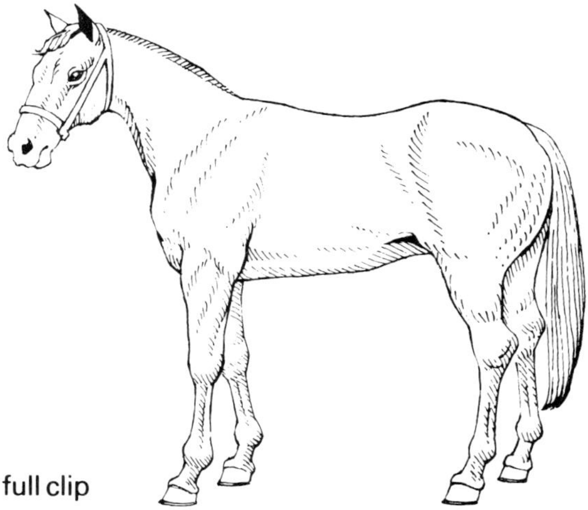

full clip

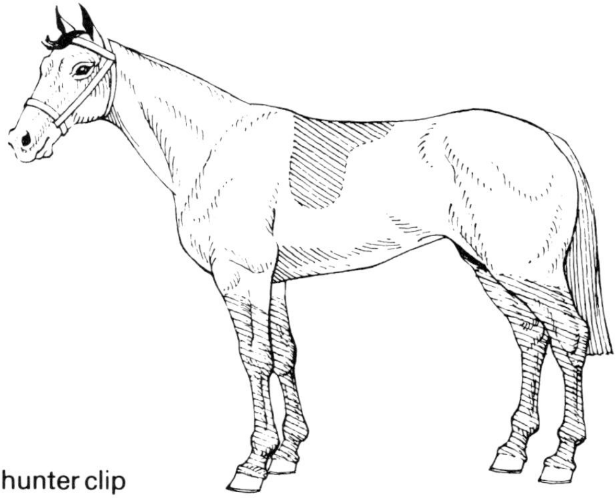

hunter clip

Sometimes hunters are clipped right out for the first clip of the season, but the hair is left on the legs and saddle patch for the second clip.

Anyone who is really skilled at clipping will be able to vary the position of the saddle patch to improve the appearance of a horse that may otherwise look short in the shoulder, or long in the back.

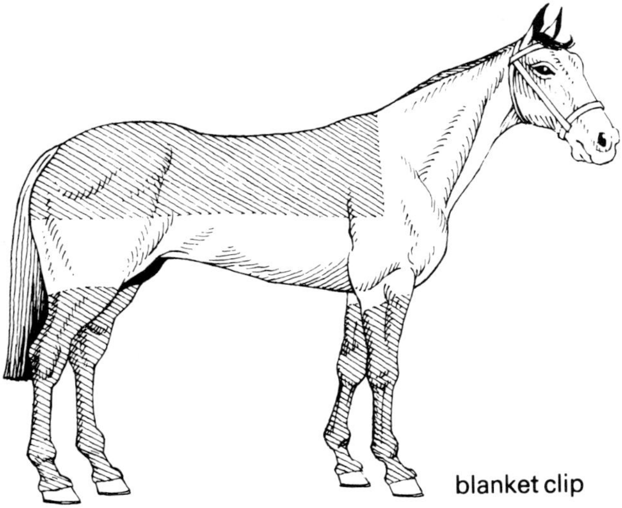

blanket clip

trace high clip

The blanket clip So named because the hair is removed from the neck and belly to enable the horse to keep cool during exercise, and the patch which is left is in the shape of a blanket.
The trace high clip This is a very handy clip for a horse left out at grass with a New Zealand rug. It is also a particularly useful clip for harness ponies. The hair is removed from beneath the neck, and also below the belly as far up as the traces, and from the legs as far as half-way down the forearm and thighs.

Before clipping can begin the horse's coat must be dry and reasonably well groomed. A twitch may be necessary if the horse gives a great deal of trouble, but patience and care are much more important, particularly with a young horse, or one which is not clipped regularly.

Hair must not be removed from the muzzle region or the ears, and care must also be taken not to clip the sides of the mane or the root of the tail. The clippers should not be used on the back of the tendons or the fetlocks.

A cold horse will become fidgety, and so it is as well to keep a rug across the loins, and if a hay net will keep him quiet, then it would be wise to give him one. Remember to move the comb and scissors upwards against the hair. Horse clippers must never be used on the tail.

The hairs of the mane and tail will need *trimming*, and they will pluck more easily when the skin is warm, and the pores are open after exercise.

Pulling is required to thin out an over-thick mane, or to reduce a long mane to the required length, so that it will lie flat. Hair should be removed a little at a time, and the longest hairs from underneath should be dealt with first. Scissors or clippers must never be used, and it is much better to pull the mane a little at a time, so that the horse does not become bored or restless.

When a mane is *hogged* all the hair is removed with the clippers. To hog correctly the horse's head needs to be lowered and the crest stretched, best done by an assistant standing in front of the horse's head and rubbing his ears until he contentedly lowers his head.

You should start by clipping the mane from the withers towards the poll, and care must be taken to make sure that no unsightly line is left where the coat meets the crest. A mane will usually need to be hogged every three weeks, and it is unlikely that a mane once hogged will ever become long again even after two or three years.

A *plaited* mane shows off the neck and crest; it looks neat, and also encourages the mane to fall on to the correct side, or offside, of the neck. There must always be an odd number of plaits along the neck, and one plait to even up the numbers on the forelock.

Some weeks after a horse has been clipped, long hairs known as 'cat hairs' will appear on various parts of the coat which will make him look rather untidy. The most usual method of removing these hairs is by *singeing*, but this task is best left to an expert.

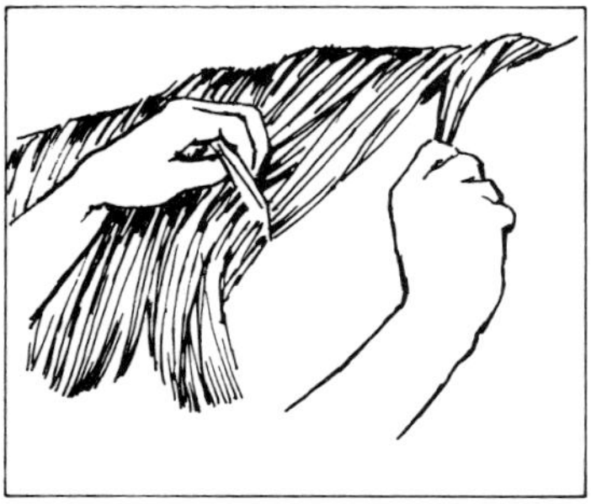

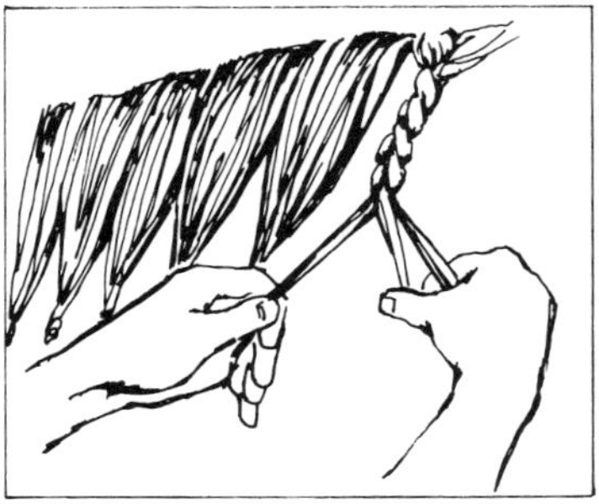

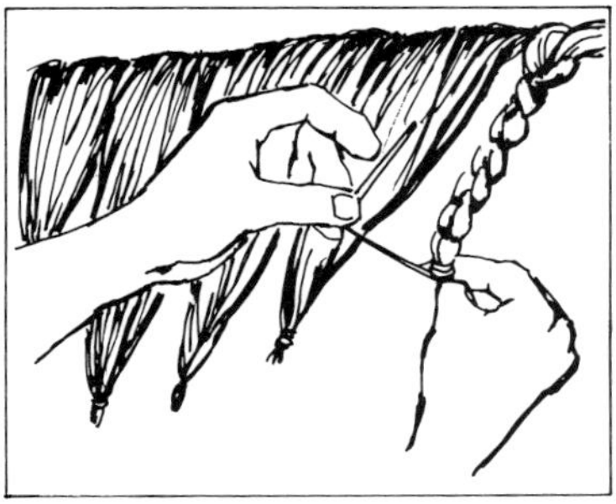

How is a horse shod?

A horse needs to be shod frequently, particularly if it has to do a considerable amount of roadwork, because otherwise the wall of the foot would wear away more quickly than it could be replaced. Even when shod, the wall will still continue to grow, and unless the shoes are removed, or replaced, at regular intervals, the wall will continue to grow until the foot becomes unduly long. The nails holding the shoe on to the foot will also become risen and these can cause cuts.

There are two systems of shoeing, *hot shoeing* and *cold shoeing*. In hot shoeing, the shoe is specially made by the blacksmith to fit the horse's foot and after being tried on hot and adjustments made until it fits perfectly, it is then cooled and nailed on securely. When a horse is cold shod, a ready-made shoe is fitted as well as possible.

Hot shoeing is obviously a far more satisfactory process, and there are six different stages – the removal of the old shoe, and the

The leather apron protects the blacksmith's legs as he drives the nails home to secure the shoe.

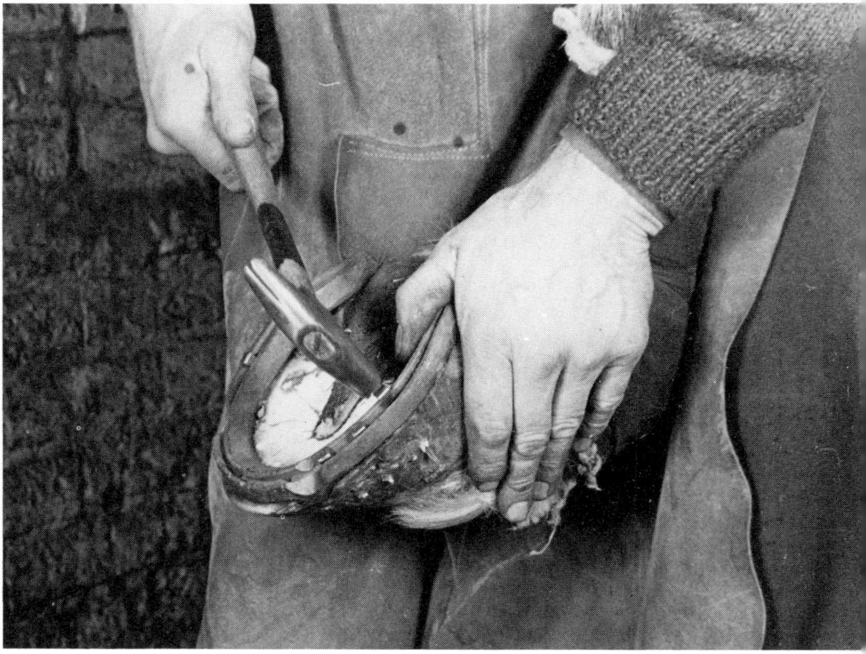

preparation, forging, fitting, nailing on, and finishing of the new.

When the blacksmith removes the old shoe, he first of all cuts all the clenches with the help of his buffer and driving hammer. He then levers the shoe off with his pincers, making sure that the wall of the foot is not damaged.

He then prepares the foot by cutting back any horn that has become overgrown, and making any adjustment of the hoof ready for the new shoe. The blacksmith cleans out the sole and frog, and makes sure that they are in good condition, and the foot is in good shape generally. Any wall that is not required is removed with a drawing knife or toeing knife or horn cutter. The rasp is then used to ensure that the foot has a level surface on which the weight of the horse can be borne.

The actual making of the new shoe is known as forging, and after the iron has been shaped, the nail holes are stamped and the clips drawn.

The fitting is carried out while the shoe is hot, and the blacksmith carries the shoe across to the horse on a 'pritchel'. By searing the horn he can make a perfect fit. This process is not at all painful to the horse, and if you watch a blacksmith at work you will see that although a horse will very often take a great deal of interest in what is going on, he never shows any signs of discomfort.

After the shoe has been cooled by being immersed in water, it is then nailed in place, and the end of the nail where it penetrates the wall is turned over and twisted off, leaving a small piece of nail projecting from the hoof which is called the clench.

The blacksmith nails the clips in position, and then finishes off by rasping the clenches smooth and imbedding them into the wall of the hoof. The rasp is finally run round the part where the horn and shoe meet, to reduce any possibility of the hoof cracking.

It is important to remember that a shoe should be made to fit the foot, and not the foot to fit the shoe.

There are various types of shoe, but the most common is known as the *hunter shoe*, which is ideally suited to a horse or pony doing fast work on grass, such as show jumping, eventing, showing and gymkhanas.

It is possible for a horse to work unshod, providing he does not have to work on hard gritty roads or flinty tracks, and every care is taken to ensure that the wall of the foot does not become too worn, so that he becomes footsore. The feet of a horse or pony working unshod will still need to receive regular attention from a blacksmith, not only to prevent splitting and cracking but also to ensure that the surface of the foot remains level.

How should you look after a horse's feet each day?

A horse's feet should be examined and cleaned out each day, because there can be few truer sayings than 'No foot, no horse'.

Pick up each foot in turn and remove any stones or dirt which may be lodged in the foot by using the point of the hoof pick, working downwards from the heel towards the toe. In this way there will be less chance of the pick damaging the soft parts of the frog in the centre of the hoof. Check by smell for any sign of problems like thrush, and run the tips of your fingers round the hoof to see whether there are any risen nails or clenches. Then tap the shoe to see whether it is secure, or whether a visit to the blacksmith may be necessary.

Always use the hoof pick from heel to toe.

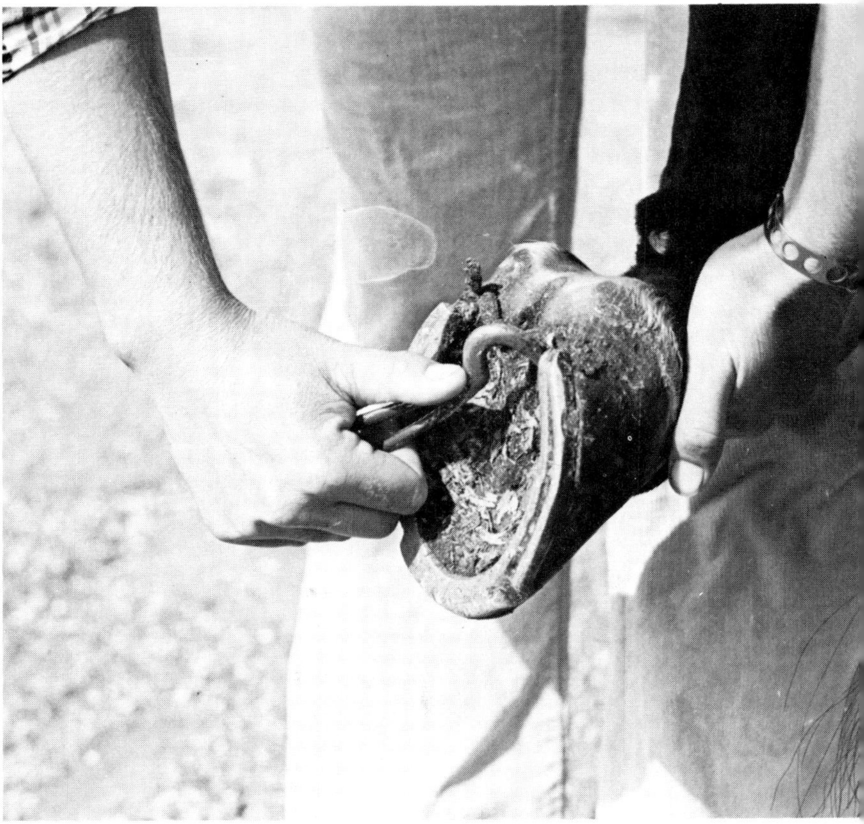

Picking up a horse's foot is not difficult providing you use the correct method. To pick up the off forefoot, stand by the horse's shoulder facing the tail, run your right hand down the forearm and take hold of the leg above the knee. Then exert pressure with your elbow until the horse's weight shifts to the opposite leg. Then lift up the leg with your left hand and take hold of the foot near the toe. The same method applies to the near forefoot.

When picking up a hind leg, stand facing the rear and run your hand down until it is just above the hock. Then take up the leg with the hand in front of the fetlock and lift the foot from the ground.

After cleaning out your horse's feet and checking the shoes, use a brush for a final oiling.

These two ponies look alert, bright-eyed and healthy.

What would you look for in a healthy horse?

A healthy horse should stand evenly on all four feet, with its forefeet square, its head up and alert, and eyes bright and wide open. Its coat should shine and the skin be soft and supple. If the coat is dull, or feels as though it is sticking to the muscles below; or if the hair is on end and not lying flat, then there is something amiss. A lot of discharge from the eye is also an indication that the horse is probably in a bad state of health. Droppings, which should be passed about eight times a day, should break on hitting the ground, and urine should be passed easily.

A horse never rests a foreleg unless there is something radically wrong, although a healthy horse will often rest a hind leg without any cause for alarm.

What would you do if you thought your horse was sick?

Like their owners, horses sometimes develop illnesses like a cold or even 'flu, and if you are worried about your horse the first thing to do is to take his temperature. The normal temperature of a horse is 38°C (100·5°F), but horses' temperatures are inclined to rise a little during the day, and it is often higher at mid-day than it is in the morning, or at night.

After taking his temperature, check his pulse. The general method is to place a finger beneath the horse's lower jaw where the heartbeats can usually easily be felt. Respirations in a healthy horse should be about ten to twelve to the minute, but should not exceed fifteen.

Any horse with a temperature or a cough, or who seems off-colour for no good reason, should be isolated if this is possible. If there is any doubt as to the cause of the trouble, or if he does not respond quickly to treatment, a veterinary surgeon should be called. Experience has shown that this is often cheaper in the long run, and there is less chance of your horse suffering permanent harm.

What minor ailments affect a horse's legs and feet?

In everyday stable life there are all sorts of minor ailments which come from the legs and feet. A frequent cause of lameness is corns, which are often caused by faulty shoeing. These are bruises to the fleshy sole between the hoof wall and the frog. If the bruise is very severe the foot may have to be poulticed, but if, as sometimes happens, the corn festers, and matter gathers in the heel, seek the advice of your veterinary surgeon.

There are many causes of lameness, from the less serious splints, which are bony growths on the cannon bone, to the very much more serious navicular disease; and from laminitis to bog spavins (see glossary).

A more frequent cause of trouble is the over-reach, which is caused by the foreleg being struck by the hind foot, causing a nasty wound either to the tendons or to the bulbs of the heels. This occurs usually when the horse is jumping, or it can happen at the gallop. The cut must be washed out with antiseptic and treated as for a bruised wound. This sort of wound can be entirely accidental or it can be caused through faulty action, or faulty shoeing behind, so it is as well to examine the hind feet. If necessary ask your farrier if he will round the inside of the hind shoes, and set them back as far as possible. If your horse is inclined to over-reach it is wise always to use over-reach boots for fast work and jumping to protect him from this type of injury.

Brushing wounds are caused by a horse striking the opposite leg on the inner part of the fetlock, or sometimes the coronet. The cause may again be bad action, ill-fitting shoes, bad conformation, old age, or even over-work. Once you have traced the cause, it may be as well to use brushing boots.

A stone lodged between the shoe and the frog can cause temporary lameness, but if the rider quickly dismounts and removes the stone there should not be any problem.

Bruised soles caused by a stone can take longer to cure. The sole becomes tender to pressure, and may show a red mark. A poultice or tubbing is usually the answer, as in the case of a pricked foot where a shoeing nail has actually penetrated the sensitive part of the foot after a visit to the blacksmith.

Cracked heels or chapping of the skin behind the pastern can cause severe lameness. They are caused by exposure to wet conditions, or neglect after the legs have been washed; you should always rub down your pony's legs after washing.

If the horse or pony is in a soft condition, girth galls can become a nuisance. They show on the soft skin behind the elbow. It is as well to leave the saddle off for a few days, and harden the skin by a daily application of salt and water or methylated spirit. A section of a rubber inner tube over the girth helps protect the sore from further rubbing.

How should a horse be given medicine?

There are six different ways of administering medicine to a horse. The simplest way is in the feed, but this is of little use if the horse is off his food. Whenever medicine in either liquid or powder form is administered in this way, the food should first be dampened.

Another easy way is in the drinking water, providing not only that

The modern way of worming is by means of a syringe, but this is not a job for the inexperienced.

the medicine will mix with water, but that the horse will be prepared to drink it.

The third method is on the tongue, but the medicine has to be mixed with something like treacle into a stiff paste, when it becomes known as *electuary*, so that it can be smeared with a smooth blunt stick either on the back of the tongue, or on the back teeth.

Horse balls, which are rather like pills or tablets, can be either blown down the throat or gently forced through the mouth with the horse's head raised. It is as well to massage the horse's neck when this is done.

Another popular way of administering medicine is by way of horse drinks. The horse's head has to be raised, and the medicine can then be administered slowly through the side of the mouth from the bottle. If he starts to cough, his head must be lowered immediately before the process can be repeated.

The other way of giving medicine is by means of an injection.

What is colic?

Colic, which is a pain in the stomach, is probably the most common of all horse ailments. It can be either a very mild attack, in which case it will pass off in an hour or two, or it can become very much more serious. It should never be treated in an off-hand fashion, because if it is not dealt with efficiently it can, and does, kill.

As soon as you realise that a horse has colic, telephone the veterinary surgeon immediately, because it may take him some time to reach the stable, and speed of action is important.

The first signs of colic are restlessness, so that the horse keeps getting up and down. He never wants to stay down for more than a minute or two at a time and when he stands up he keeps on looking around at his flank and trying to kick his own stomach. There are many other symptoms, but the moment you suspect that a horse is suffering from colic, keep the horse warm but walk him around, and try and prevent him from getting down on the ground and rolling.

Always try and find the cause of the colic, but usually it can be traced to bad stable management, such as watering after a feed; overeating when tired; feeding a horse poor quality food that might have gone off; sudden changes in diet; getting a horse chilled after fast work; leaving him in the stable when he is hot, or even neglecting to have a horse's teeth seen to regularly so that he is unable to masticate his food properly.

Saddlery and equipment

What are the most important rugs for a stable?

Every stable requires at least one rug, and if horses are stabled in winter, rugs and blankets will be necessary in order to maintain body warmth. There are many different rugs which are designed for different occasions.

When buying rugs it is important to get the correct size, and measurements are taken from the centre of the horse's chest to where the rug should reach on the horse's quarters. This is because the actual measurement size of the rug is the length from where the rug buckles in front to the back edge.

All rugs must fit comfortably at the withers and allow plenty of freedom of movement across the chest. The end of the rug should come within 10 cm (4 inches) of the horse's tail.

The Night rug is essential for a stabled horse in winter.

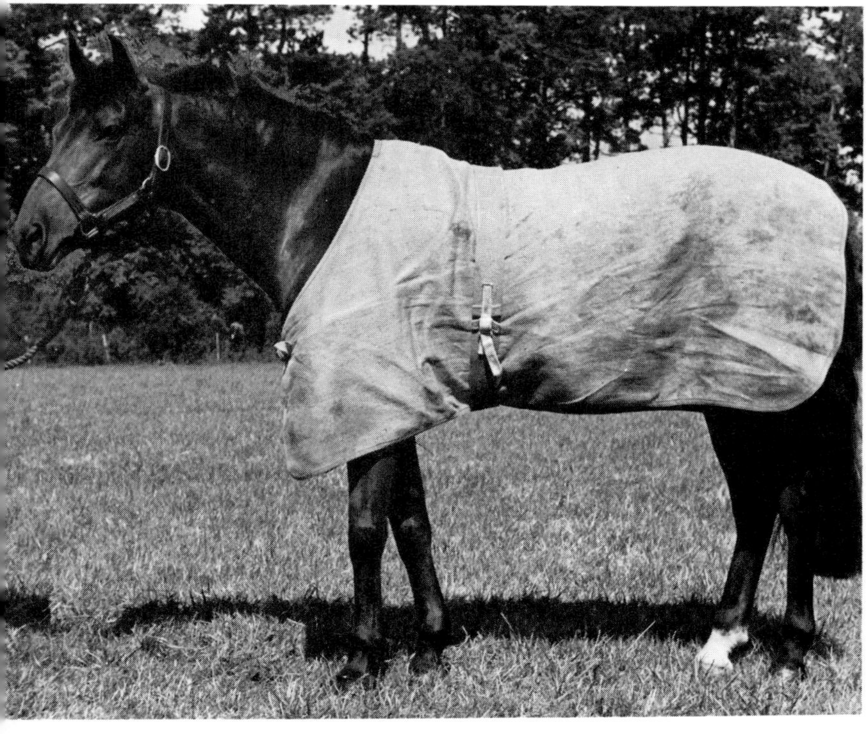

Night rug Of the different types of rugs, the most useful is the night rug or *stable rug*. This is made of strong jute or canvas and is lined with blanket. A good quality rug, if kept clean and repaired, will stand a great deal of wear and tear. Some rugs are lined at the withers, but if not, a piece of sheepskin sewn into the rug will prevent unnecessary rubbing.

In winter, when the weather is particularly cold, a good warm blanket will be needed under the rug. Good quality blankets can mean a saving in food, because if he is being kept warm by the blanket, a horse will not need to use up so much food in order to maintain body heat.

Day rug A woollen day rug with the owner's initials is perhaps rather a luxury, but it does look very smart, particularly when travelling or at shows. There are many qualities of rugging used for day rugs, and it pays to buy the best, because the poor quality rugs just do not last. Sometimes these rugs have a matching hood which covers the head and neck, and has coverings for the ears and holes in the front, cut out of the hood, for the horse to look through.

The day rug should be fitted with a *fillet string* at the rear to prevent the rug from blowing up in the wind. The fillet string is made of plaited braid to match the rug's binding, and it passes across the horse's quarters, beneath the tail, and just above the hocks.

Summer sheets These are made of either cotton or linen and take the place of day rugs during the summer months; like day rugs they can have the owner's initials sewn into the corners. The summer sheet is not intended to keep a horse warm, but to keep down the coat, and to keep away the dust and flies. It can be useful to keep draughts off the horse's loins when travelling, particularly when put over a string *sweat sheet*, and kept in place with a roller.

Lavenham nylon rugs and sheets These are becoming very popular for stable use because they are light and easily washed. They are made in a variety of colours and bindings and are fitted with a fillet string and surcingle.

Areborn rug A very useful item of stable equipment is the Areborn rug or *sweat sheet* which is rather like a string vest and works on the same principle, by keeping pockets of warm air between the horse's skin and the outer covering. It should be kept in place with a surcingle or roller, because horses when warm have a tendency to roll, and it is easy for them to get their legs caught up in the holes. It should always be used with another rug or sheet over the top because otherwise there is a very real chance of a horse becoming chilled across the loins.

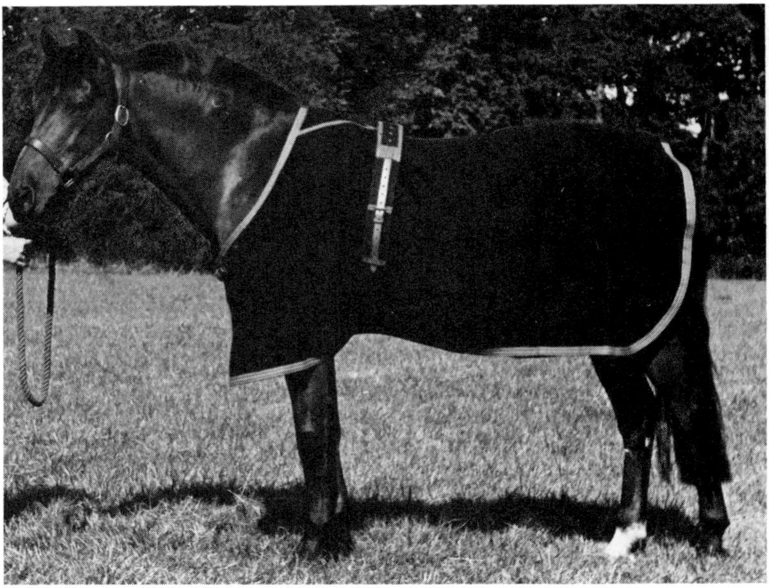

The Day rug is made of wool and looks very smart.

Summer sheets keep away dust and flies.

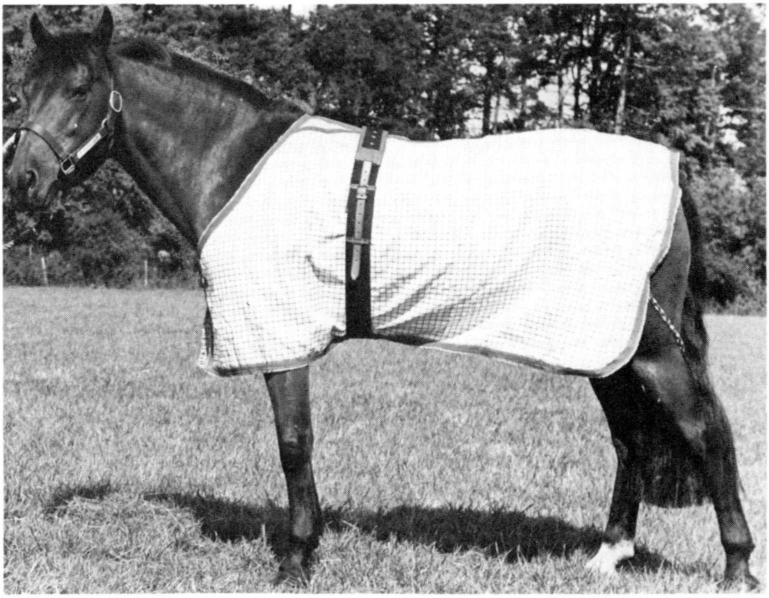

Lavenham rugs are light and easy to wash.

The sweat sheet is rather like a string vest.

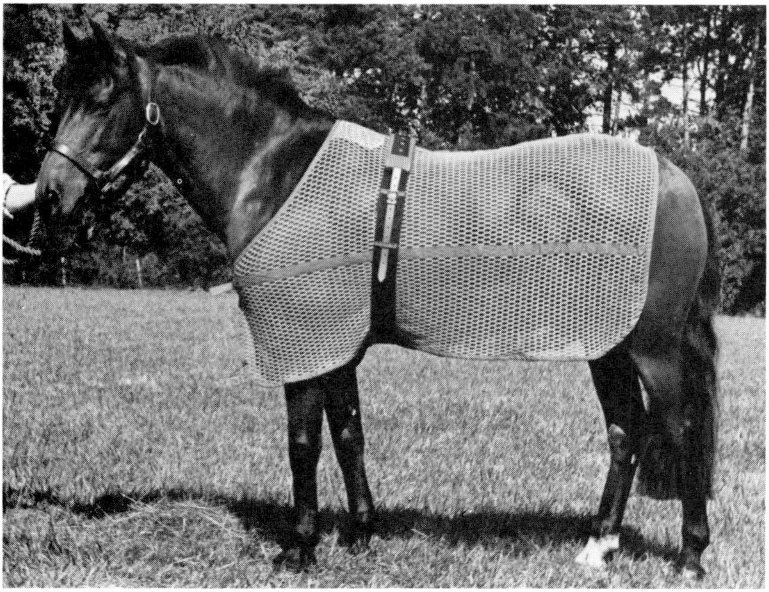

New Zealand rugs Although these are usually only used when horses or ponies are kept at grass all or part of the time during the winter, they are a very useful addition to the stable. Horses love being free to roll and nibble some grass even in winter, and in days when the weather is warm enough it can be very beneficial to a stable horse to be turned out for an hour or so with a New Zealand rug for protection.

These are waterproof rugs, usually made of canvas or nylon with leg straps that fasten round the hind legs to keep them in place when a horse gets down to roll. If a horse is turned out, the New Zealand rug must be removed and put on again at least once a day. The wither section of the rug should be padded for protection against chafing. When removing the rug it is important to unclip the leg straps first.

The art of 'rugging-up' is a skill which comes with practice, and is easily acquired if one knows the right way. Rugs and blankets are extremely expensive and it is worthwhile taking good care of them. There is no excuse for dirty rugs, although some staining is inevitable during the winter, or when a horse is stalled at night.

First unclip the leg straps of a New Zealand rug.

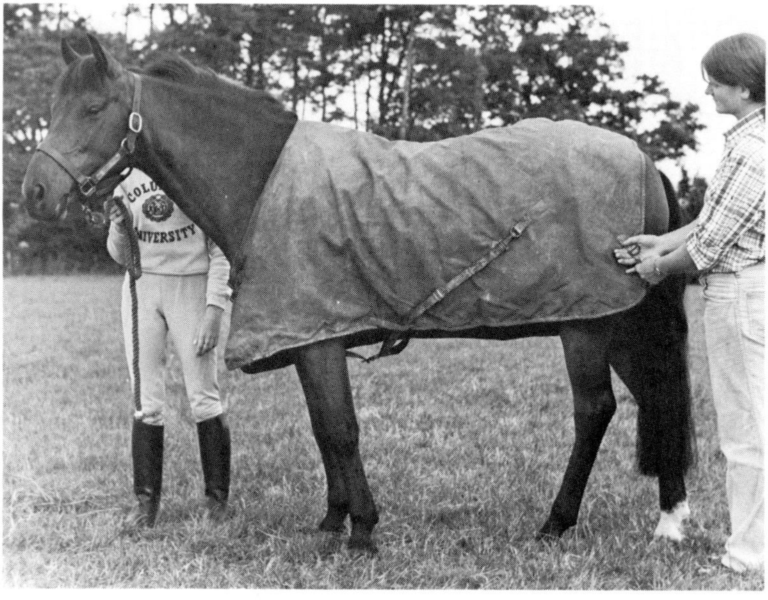

What is a surcingle and a roller?

Every rug needs some form of surcingle or roller in order to keep it in place. *Surcingles*, usually made of various types of webbing such as jute, wool, cotton or hemp, are long lengths of material with a leather strap at one end and a buckle at the other. Sometimes the surcingle is stitched to the rug, but it is important to ensure that it does not put undue pressure on the spine.

A *roller* is really a surcingle with a built-in pad that rests either side of the spine. Rollers are never sewn into a rug, and although they are fitted with their own padding it is as well to cut up a square of foam rubber to place between the withers and the roller.

If a *tail guard* is used the strap will have to be looped through the roller and buckled into place.

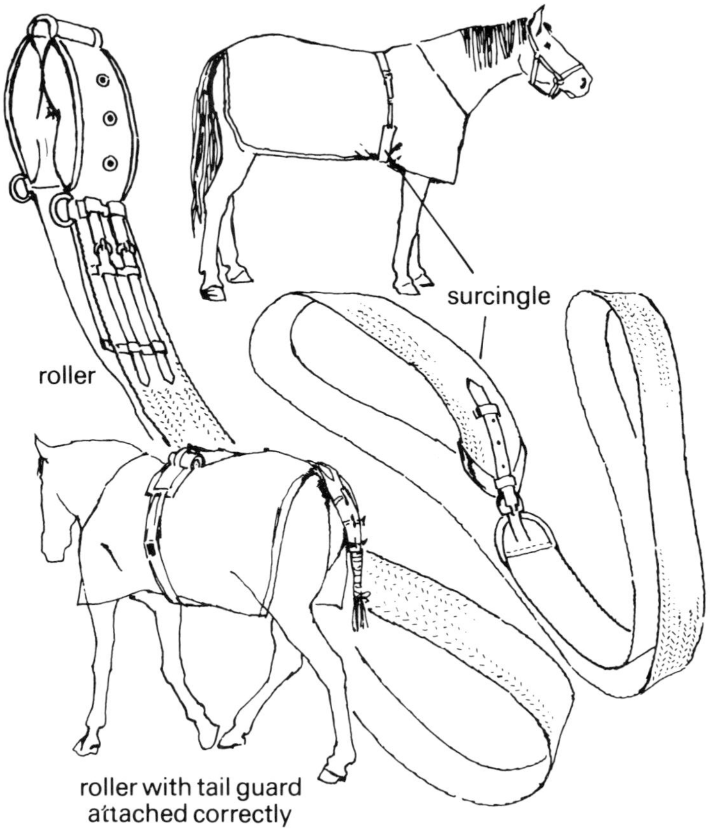

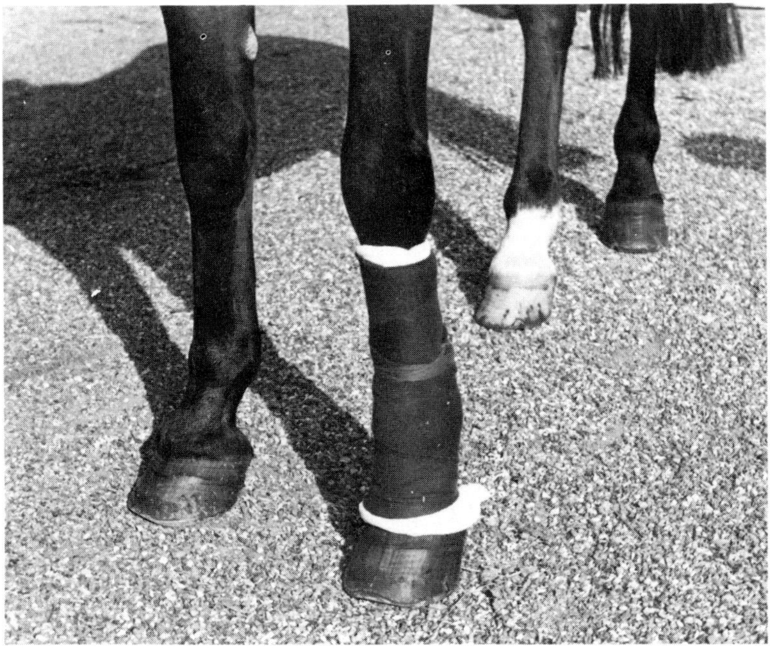

Stable bandages are made of wool and must not be tight.

What are the main stable bandages?

Bandages have a wide variety of uses apart from providing warmth and comfort. They can provide protection against injury when travelling, help prevent legs from filling, or help dry off wet legs, when put on over straw.

Stable bandages These are made of wool and must be carefully applied to prevent injury through being too tight. Before putting on a bandage make sure that it is correctly rolled with the tapes neatly folded up inside.

When putting on a stable bandage start just below the knee or hock, and pass the bandage round the leg in even turns. When the coronet is reached start to bandage again in an upward direction, so that the bandage ends at the starting point. The tapes should be tied so that the knots lie either to the inside or the outside of the leg, and not to the front where they will press on to the bone, or behind where they can press on to the tendons. The tapes should be tied in a double bow, and the ends tucked into the folds of the bandage.

Exercising bandages These are sometimes called pressure or support bandages; they are 6 to 7 cm ($2\frac{1}{2}$ to 3 inches) wide and made of stockinette or crepe. They are used to support the tendons at the back of the legs, to reinforce weak or strained tendons, and to protect the legs from thorns and brambles. Exercise bandages are applied with a considerable amount of firmness over a thick layer of cotton wool from just below the knee to just above the fetlock joint. Care must be taken, however, to ensure that they do not interfere with the action of the joint.

When the bandages are removed the back tendons and fetlocks should be given a brisk rub with the palms of the hands to ensure that the circulation is working properly. Never kneel to put on, or take off, bandages. A bending or crouching position is much safer.

Exercise or support bandages are used to support tendons and protect against thorns or brambles.

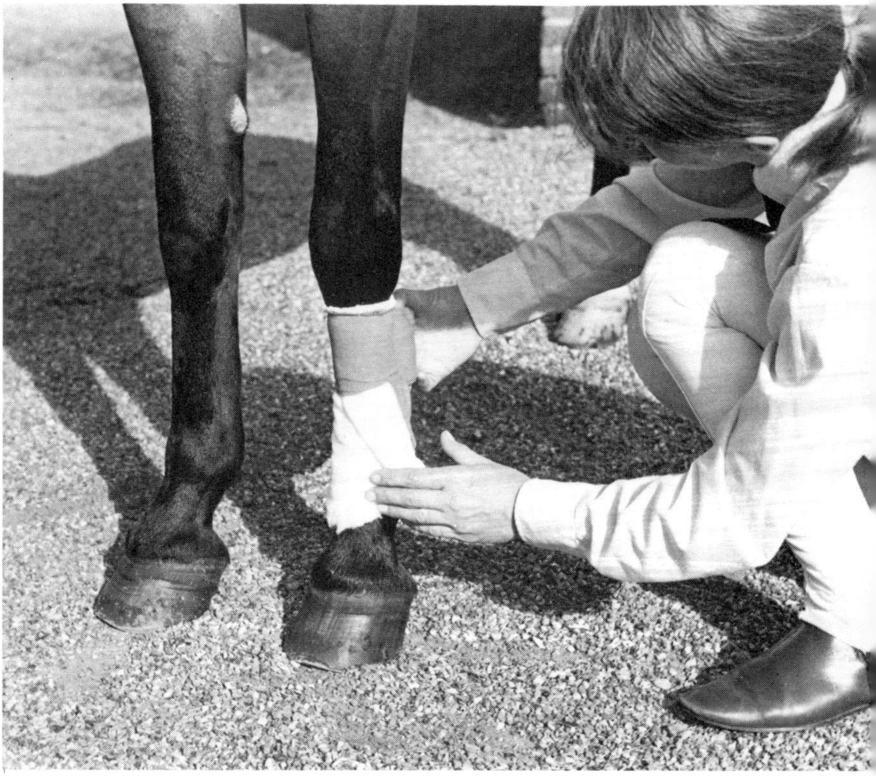

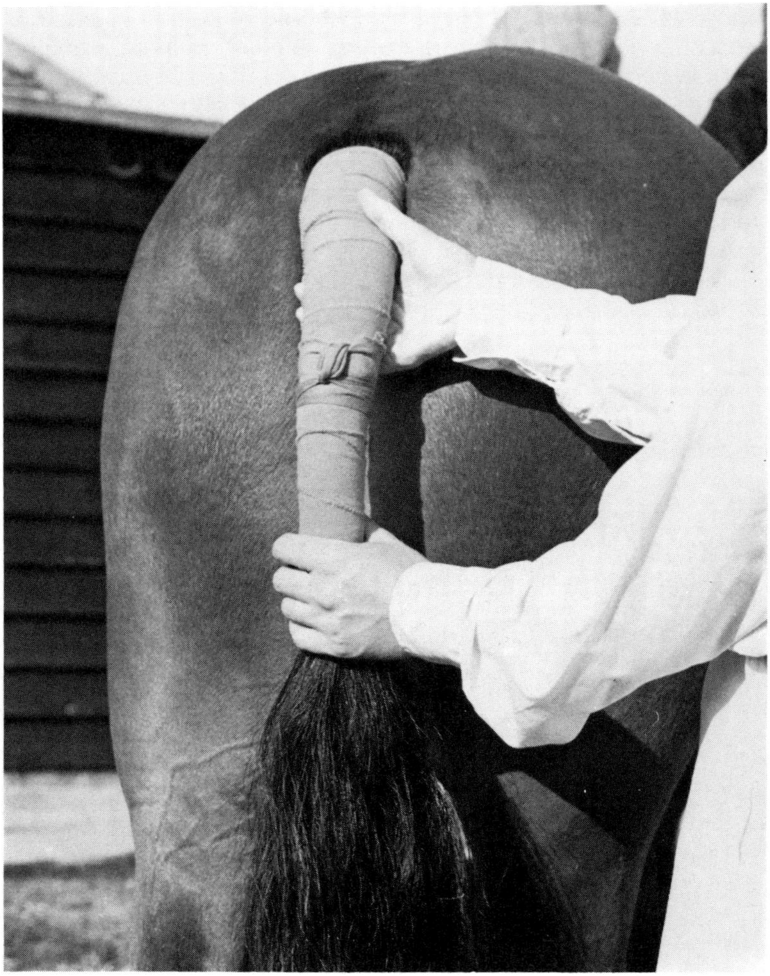

To remove a tail bandage grasp it very near the dock and slide it downwards off the tail.

Tail bandages Like exercising bandages, these are made of stockinette or crepe about 6 to 7 cm ($2^1/_2$ to 3 inches) wide. They are used to protect the tail from injury, or from being rubbed during travelling. They also improve the appearance of the tail and help keep the hairs in position.

Always remember that tail bandages should never be used too frequently, and must never be left on overnight. Before putting on a tail bandage dampen the hairs at the top of the tail with a water brush. Raise the tail with the left hand and, leaving about 20 cm (8 inches) of the end of the bandage loose, unroll the bandage evenly round the tail working slowly downwards. Secure the spare end, and when the bandage reaches about half-way down the tail start to work upwards again until the tapes can be tied neatly near the top, and tucked away under one of the folds.

To remove the tail bandage, grasp it firmly with both hands near the dock and slide it downwards off the tail.

Tie the tapes of the tail bandage neatly but only tightly enough to ensure firmness. The tail can then be bent into shape.

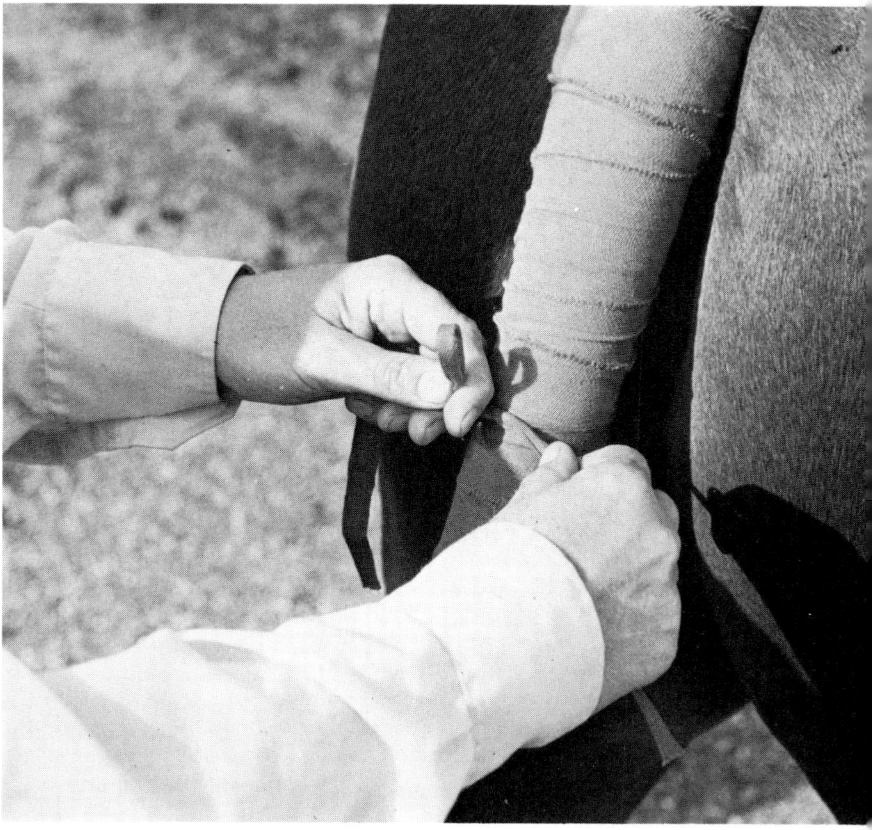

This hunting saddle gives security and comfort.

What should you look for in a saddle?

The saddle is obviously one of the most important items of equipment for every horseman and it is particularly important to ensure that it is not only a good fit for the horse but also comfortable for the rider. A saddle should be shaped so as to assist the rider to sit in the middle, or lowest part, of the seat of the saddle.

Saddles are built on frames called saddle-trees which are usually made of beech wood, but some saddles now have plastic trees. If the saddle becomes damaged, and the tree becomes broken, it must be repaired before the saddle is used again, because a saddle with a broken tree can injure a horse's back.

The stirrup leathers, which can be adjusted in length according to the rider's requirements, are fitted on to the saddle by being passed round a stirrup bar. This usually has a hinge with a point that can be turned up to prevent the leathers from slipping off the saddle when the horse is being led without a rider. It is important, however, to ensure that the points are never in the turned up position when the horse is being ridden.

Saddles are either full panelled or half panelled. A full panel is fully lined and reaches almost all the way to the bottom of the saddle flap. It has a short sweat-flap, or under-flap, between the panel and the girth tabs. A half panel reaches halfway down the saddle flap, and has a much larger sweat-flap. Half panelled saddles are particularly useful for younger riders because they enable a rider's knee and lower leg to get closer to the horse's or pony's sides.

Three types of linings are used on full panel and half panel saddles. Serge linings are absorbent, but they are also difficult to keep clean, and not very hard wearing. Linen, on the other hand, wears longer, dries quickly, and is easier to keep clean. The best lining material, however, is leather, which is easy to clean and has excellent wearing properties.

What are the main parts of a saddle called?

It is important to be able to name the parts of a saddle, and the following three diagrams will help you to memorise them more easily.

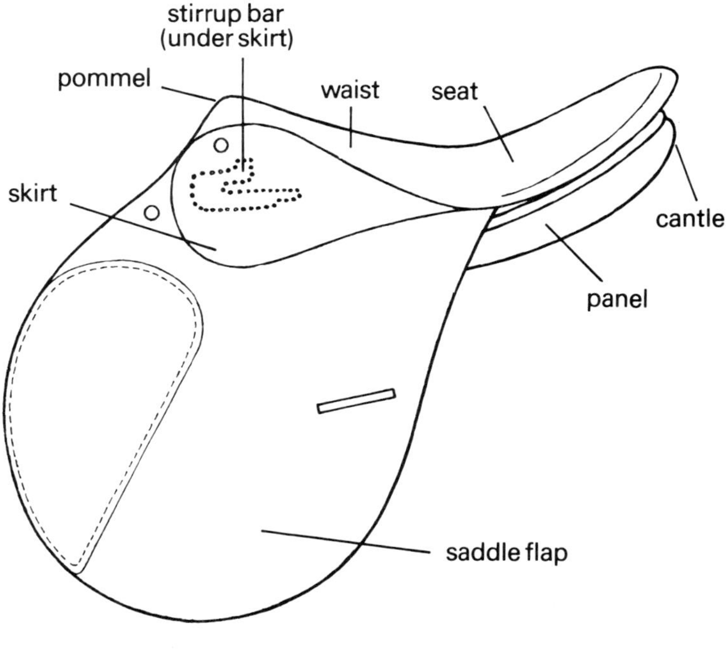

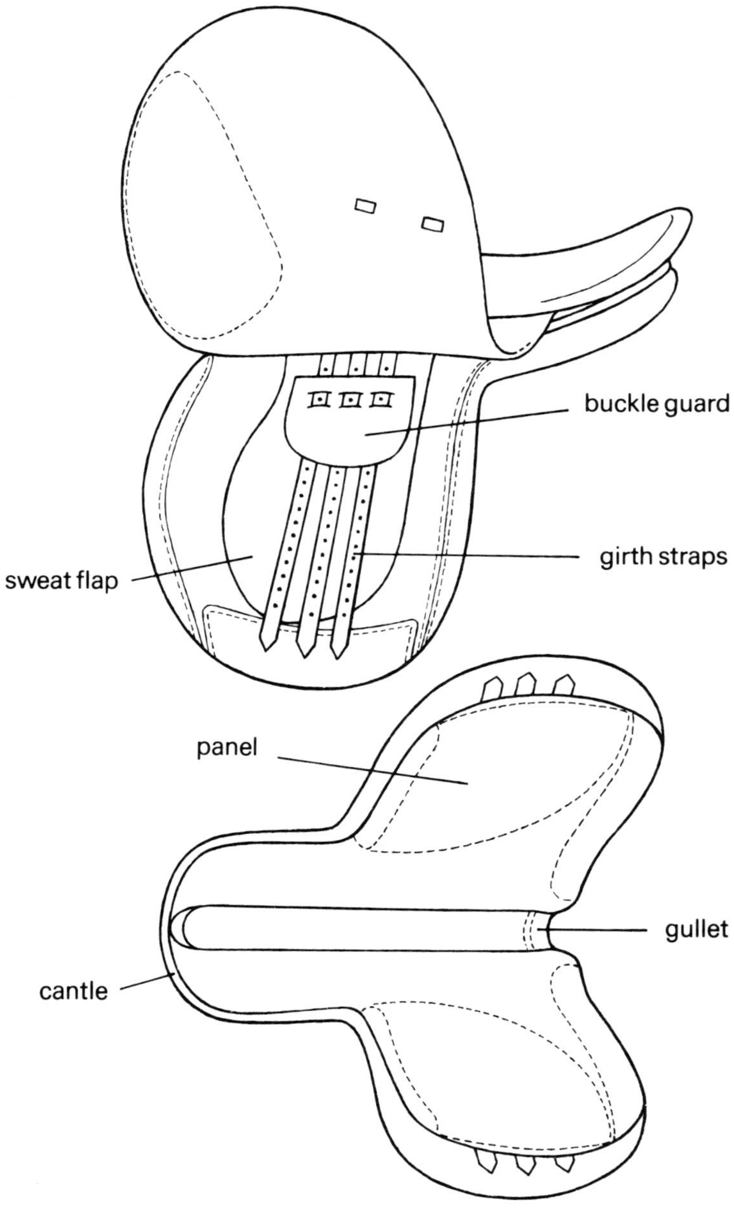
buckle guard
girth straps
sweat flap
panel
gullet
cantle

How should a saddle be fitted?

Great care must be taken to ensure that the saddle fits the horse properly. There must not be any pressure on the horse's spine, and when the rider is mounted, check the area of the cantle at the rear of the saddle. There should not be any weight on the horse's loins, and the weight of the saddle must be evenly distributed on the muscles which cover the upper part of the horse's rib cage. A badly fitting saddle can cause problems which will lay a horse or pony up for some considerable time.

It is also important to make sure that the pommel, or front of the saddle, does not press down on the horse's withers because the front arch is either too wide or too low, or pinch the withers because the arch is too narrow.

Every saddle needs checking at least once a year by the saddler who will test all the stitching and re-stuff the panels if necessary. If you are worried as to whether the saddle is pinching, use a foam numnah, and get the saddle checked by an expert as quickly as possible.

Obviously it is important to ensure that the saddle is not so large that it can hamper the play of the shoulder blades; or so small that it will be uncomfortable for the rider. Jockeys sometimes have to use very small and light saddles, but they are only in them for a short space of time.

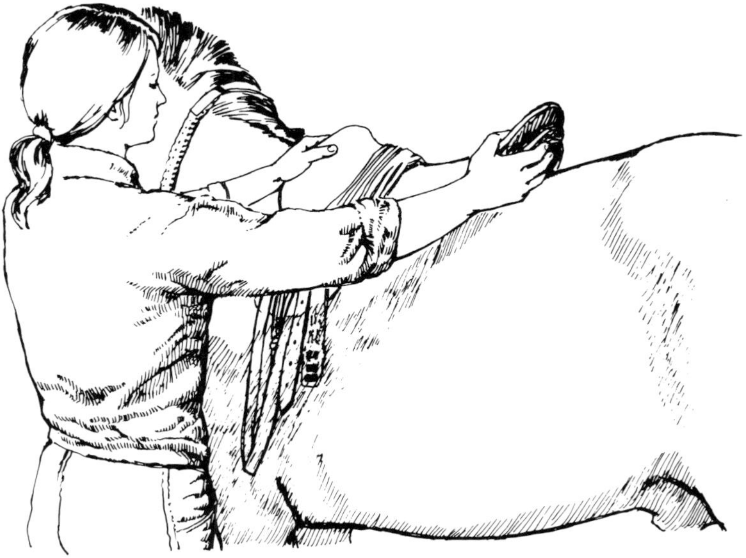

What are the best types of girth?

There are four main types of girth – string, nylon, web and leather – and by far the most popular are the string and leather varieties.

Web girths Rarely used nowadays because they can snap without warning, and they do not wear very well. They are also difficult to clean so that they remain looking smart. Single web girths should never be used because of their tendency to break.

String girths These have a number of good features. They last well and are easy to clean. They are less likely to slip on an unclipped horse and, more important, they help prevent galling, because air can get through between the strands of string that go to make up the body of the girth.

Nylon girths Rather like string girths, but they tend to stretch and slip more easily.

Leather girths Excellent providing they are kept clean and supple. They are usually made up of three-fold leather, and a simple way of keeping the leather soft is to put a strip of well-oiled cloth out of sight between the folds.

Girths should be of the correct length for the saddle and the horse. It is important to ensure that there are at least two spare holes above the buckle on each side when the saddle is in place, because girths usually need to be tightened once the rider has been in the saddle for a few moments and the horse has stopped blowing himself out.

web girths

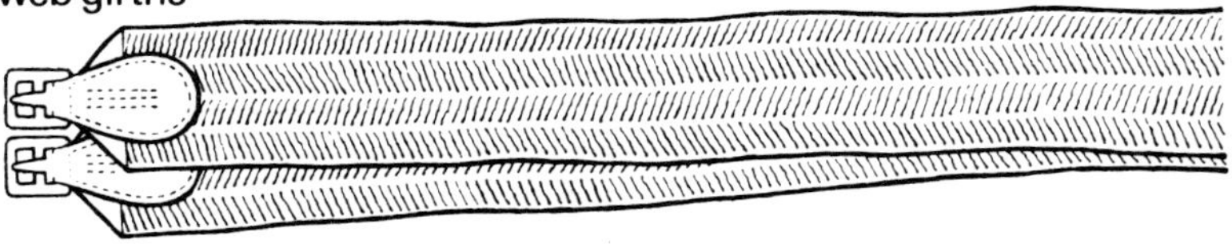

nylon girth

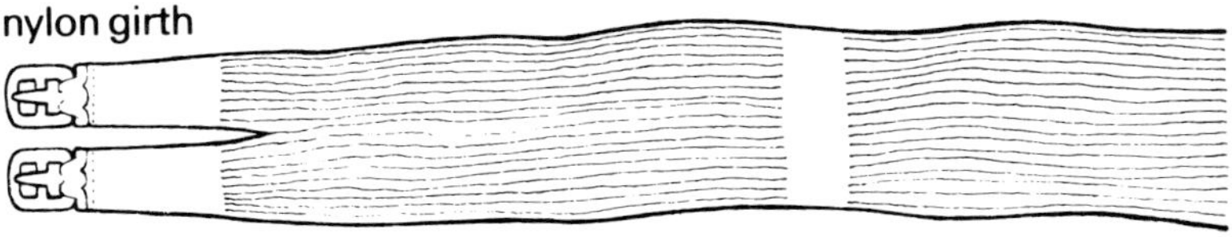

leather girth

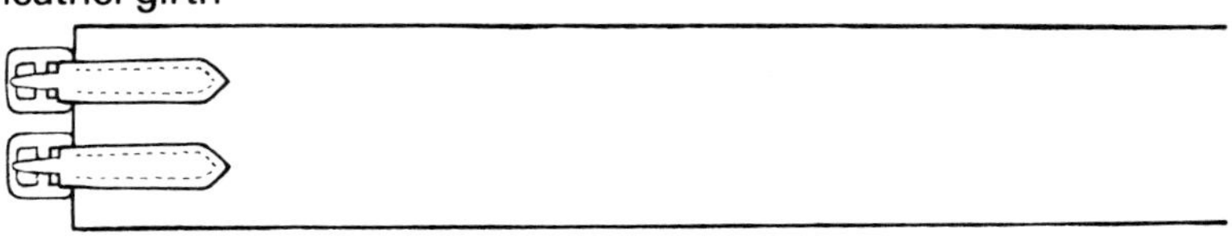

This safety stirrup is useful for very young riders.

What are the best stirrup irons?

It is most important to make certain the stirrup irons are always of best quality metal. Never buy irons made of pure nickel, because the metal is soft and the irons can bend. Steel is the safest and irons made of hand-forged stainless steel are probably the best you can buy.

Stirrup irons should never be too small for the rider's boot, and at least a centimetre (half an inch) of freedom between either side of the boot and the sides of the stirrup is essential for safety.

Some young riders use safety stirrups which have a rubber band along one side. There are varying opinions on whether the section with the rubber band should be worn on the inside, to prevent the band from becoming undone if a twig or branch gets between the stirrup and the boot, or on the outside to prevent the rider's ankle from turning inwards.

They are not entirely satisfactory and do not hang straight because they are obviously heavier on one side than the other. It is, however, important that the metal used is of the best because of this weakness.

Which bridle?

Careful attention must be paid to the bridle and also to the type and size of bit to be used, if the horse and rider are to enjoy each other's company.

The bridle is divided into several parts and it is important to learn the names of each part by heart. The following diagrams will help you to do so.

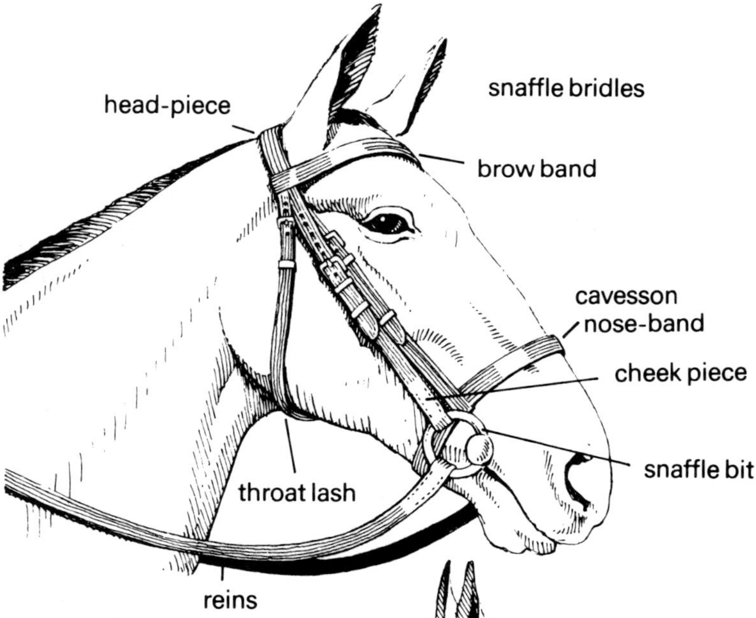

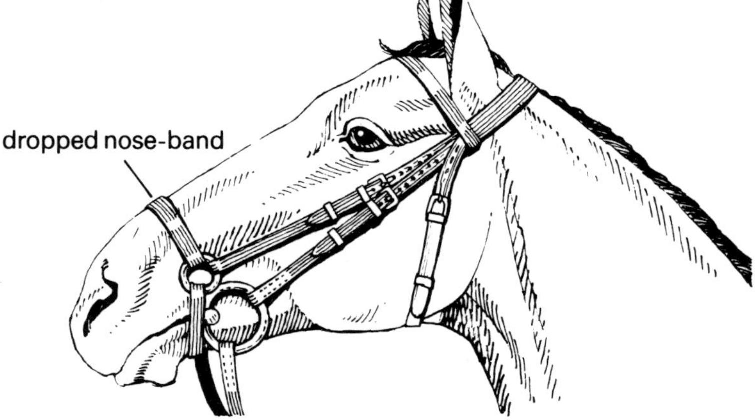

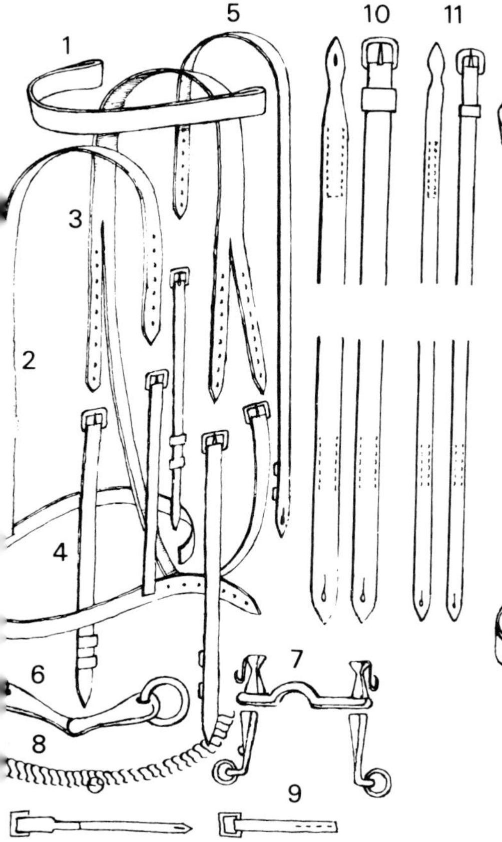

1 brow band
2 nose-band
3 head-piece
4 cheek pieces
5 bridoon cheek and sliphead
6 bridoon (snaffle) bit
7 Weymouth (curb) bit
8 curb chain
9 lip strap
10 snaffle reins
11 curb reins

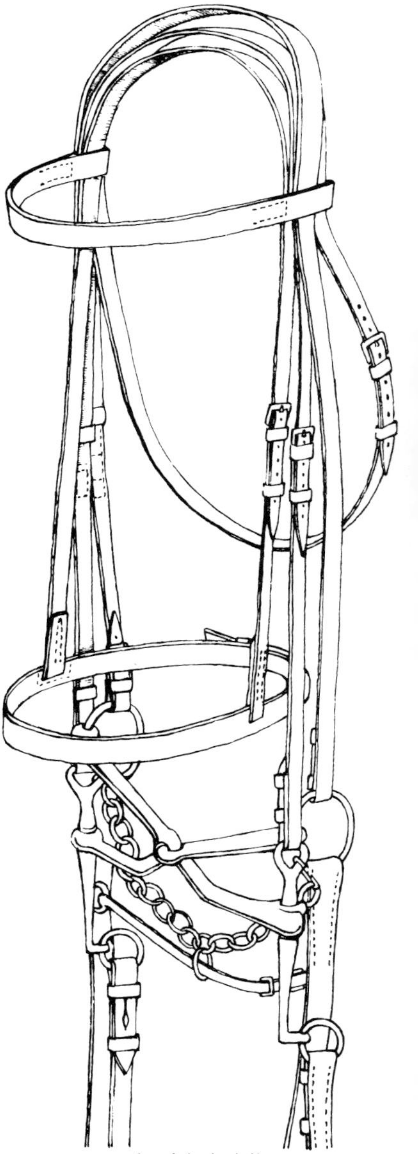

double bridle

The golden rule to remember with all forms of 'tack' is the plainer the better. Never do away with a workmanlike appearance for the sake of anything that is flashy or gaudy.

There are various bits in common use, but the four main types are the *snaffle, kimblewick, pelham* and the *double*. The snaffle

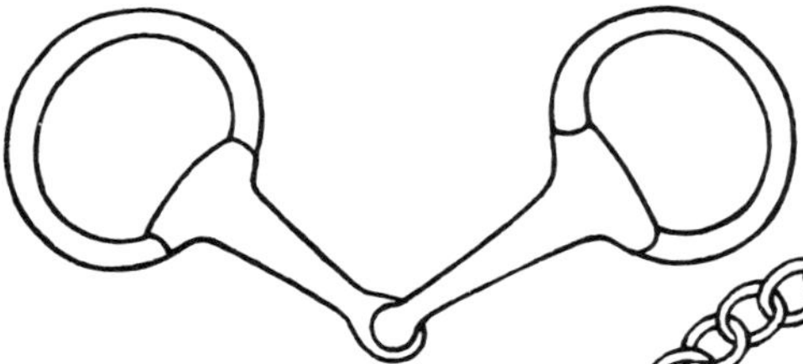

eggbutt snaffle bit

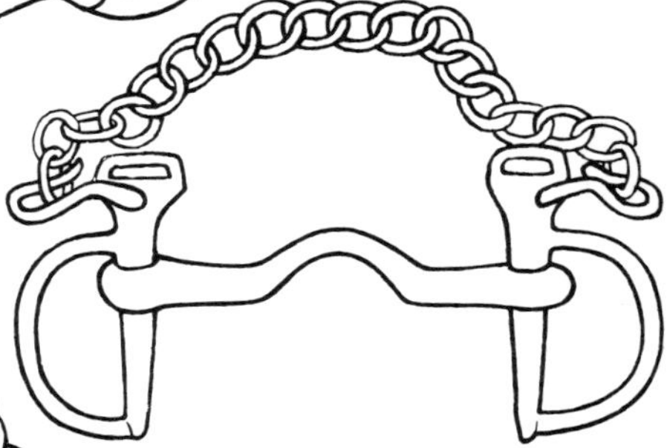

Kimblewick bit

Pelham bit

Weymouth (curb) bit and chain

and kimblewick are both used with single reins, and the pelham and the double bridle both need double reins which make them less suitable for the novice.

There are types of *bitless bridles* which, as their name suggests, means that they don't use a bit at all. They are useful if a horse has an injury to its mouth, or in some cases when a horse or pony has a particularly tender mouth, but great care must be taken in their use, and to ensure that they are fitted correctly.

Take a good look at these four types of bit and memorise the differences between them.

How should a bridle be fitted?

Care should be taken before setting off on a ride to make sure that all the parts of the bridle and the bit are fitting properly. When a bridle has been cleaned the buckles are not always replaced in the correct holes, and a badly fitting bridle is sure to lead to trouble.

The *throat lash* should never be tight. It is there to make sure that the bridle does not slip over the horse's head, but a tight throat lash, or throat latch as it is sometimes called, will interfere with a horse's breathing and its ability to flex its head.

The *brow band* must not touch the ears but should lie evenly below them. Its purpose is to prevent the head-piece from slipping back, and so the length of the brow band is important, because if it is either too long or too short the head-piece will not hang correctly.

The *cavesson nose-band* should be big enough and loose enough to allow the horse to open his mouth and flex his jaw. It should lie about half-way between the bottom of the cheek-bone and the corners of the mouth, and allow two fingers breadth between the nose-band and the front of the horse's face. A standing martingale or a lead rein is sometimes fastened to the cavesson nose-band.

The *dropped nose-band* has become very popular because it can be adjusted to prevent a horse from crossing his jaw or opening his mouth wide. Care must be taken however to make sure that it is not too tight to prevent the jaw from being flexed, and the front of the nose-band must be well above the nostrils, with the rear part fitting into the chin groove.

The *bit* should not be high enough to wrinkle the lips, and should be sufficiently wide not to pinch. If it is too wide, however, it can bruise the sides of the mouth by moving from side to side. When a double bridle is being fitted the *bridoon* should be above the bit.

The *curb chain* should lie flat in the chin groove. It should first be linked at one end over the offside hook. Then from the nearside the chain should be twisted to the right until all the links fall into place, and the chain becomes flat. Place the base of the end link on the near-side hook with the thumb uppermost, and then the link required for the correct fitting can be placed over the hook with the thumb underneath. Check that the curb chain comes into play when the cheeks of the bit are drawn back at 45 degrees to the angle of the mouth.

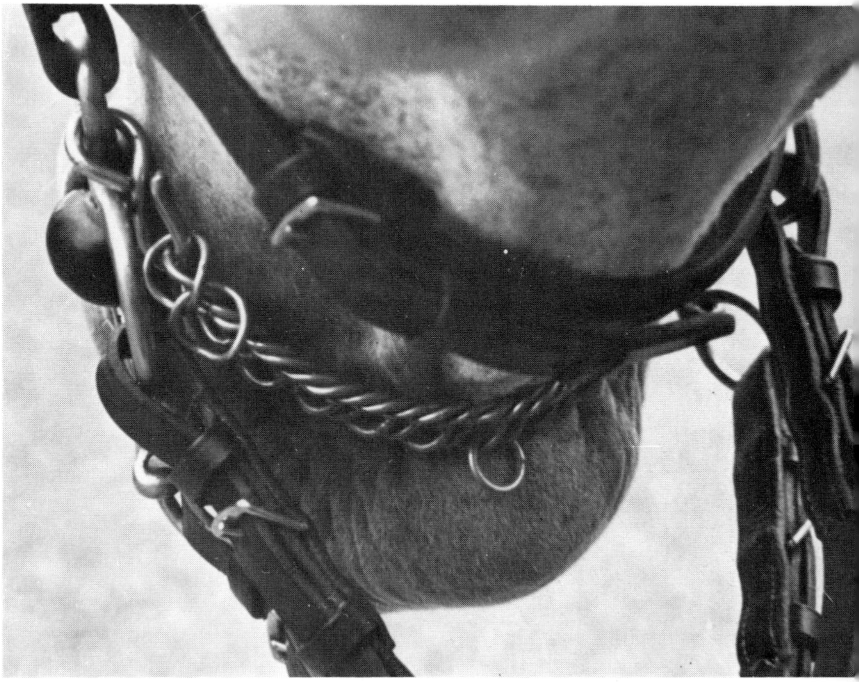

The curb chain must lie flat along the chin groove.

Left: The grakle noseband must be carefully fitted with a snaffle bit.

The *lip strap* does not need to be tight, but it must pass through the link provided for it on the curb chain. It is there to hold the chain if, for any reason, it becomes unhooked.

After checking the pieces of the bridle and the correct fitting of the bit, run your fingers under the head-pieces to make sure that they are not twisted and that the mane is lying flat.

How should tack be looked after?

All saddlery is expensive and requires regular cleaning. While doing this, it is as well to check that all the stitching is firm, and that the bits are smooth, and do not have any sharp edges or protrusions which could cause a sore mouth.

Tack cleaning can be an enjoyable job, and if the weather is fine there is no reason why it can't be done in the open air, providing you have somewhere to hang the bridle, and something to act as a saddle-horse.

Properly cleaned and well fitting saddlery not only adds to the appearance of a horse, it also makes the rider feel more comfortable.

Leather in particular gets dry and will crack unless it is kept pliable. Castor oil, dubbin, olive oil, glycerine and neatsfoot oil are all good for leather, but good quality saddle soap contains the necessary amount of suitable ingredients to keep saddlery in good order. Never use linseed or mineral oil because it will become too hard. If saddlery has to be stored, give it a good going over with Vaseline, which will not dry or become decomposed on exposure to the air.

Never use hot water or soda and never try to dry leather too quickly.

The following materials are useful for a cleaning session depending on what sort of tack you are using.

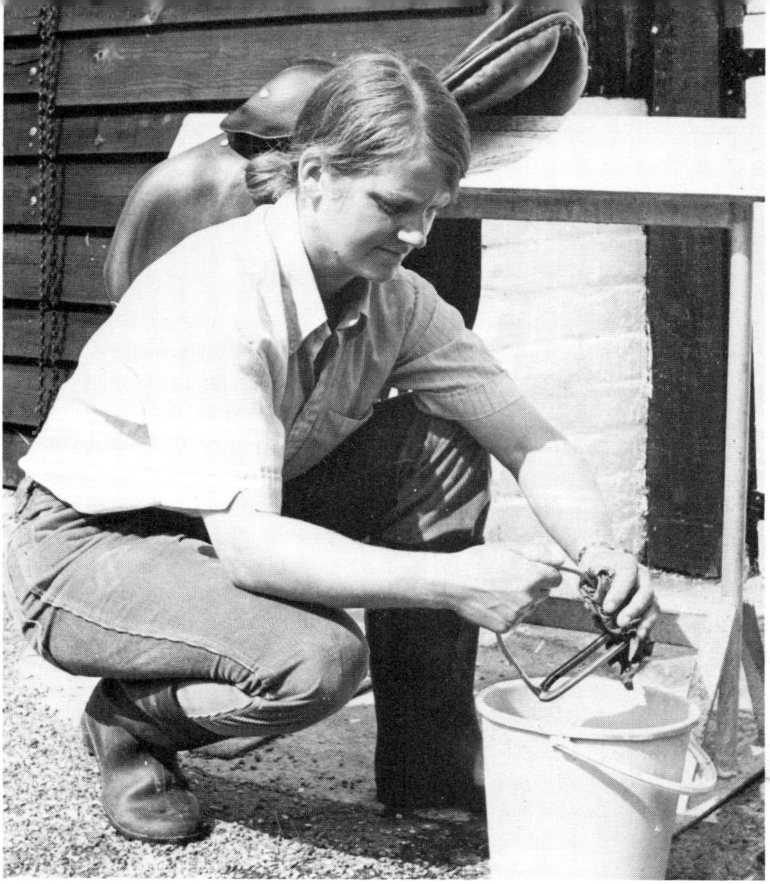

In fine weather tack can be cleaned out of doors.

1 Two sponges, one for washing over the tack and the other, a smaller sponge, for putting saddle soap on the leather.
2 A leather for drying.
3 A bar or tin of saddle soap.
4 A stable rubber or other large cloth for drying the bits and stirrup irons.
5 Some metal polish with a cloth for putting it on, and a duster for polishing it off.
6 A dandy brush for cleaning the sweat from serge linings or web girths.
7 A sharp pointed instrument for cleaning curb hooks and the D's of lip straps.
8 A bucket of warm water.

First place the saddle on a saddle-horse and remove the girths, stirrup leathers and irons, and the girth buckle guards.

The lining is the first part to be cleaned. If it is made of linen, either sponge or scrub off all the dirt and scurf, and stand the saddle up to dry. A serge lining needs to be dried and then given a thorough brushing with a dandy brush. A leather lining is more easily cleaned by holding the saddle pommel down over a bucket of cold or warm water, and rubbing it clean with a sponge. It can be

Regular saddle soaping is important to keep a saddle supple.

dried with a chamois leather, and then gone over with saddle soap.

After the saddle has been put back on to the saddle-horse it needs to be thoroughly washed with plain water, including outside and underneath the flaps. It can then be dried with a damp leather and liberally coated with saddle soap. The soap should be put on with a circular movement until it becomes absorbed into the leather.

The same should be done with the girths and stirrup leathers and the girth buckle guards.

Web, string and nylon girths need brushing daily. They can be washed occasionally with soap and water and a weak solution of ammonia. Leather girths can be washed and saddle-soaped.

The stirrup irons also need to be washed thoroughly and polished with metal polish, or silver sand in the case of plain steel.

All the buckles should also be cleaned with metal polish, but before the saddle is used again the seat and outside flaps should be rubbed over with a moist sponge and dried off with the leather. This will prevent dust, or any surplus soap, from dirtying the rider's breeches.

The bridle and other items of saddlery like the martingale have to be taken to pieces and cleaned thoroughly. Hang up the bridle on a hook. Remove the curb chain and the bit and put them into a bucket of water. Clean, dry and then polish them thoroughly. Metal polish can be used, but steel bits will need to be burnished.

After the bridle and the martingale, if one is being used, have been taken to pieces, wash the leather thoroughly with a sponge, and then dry with a damp chamois leather. Then saddle-soap all the pieces with a sponge and put the bridle together again, making sure that the buckles are in their proper places, and the strap ends are placed in their keepers and runners. Remember that keepers are the stitched loops and runners are the loops that can slide freely up and down the straps.

Finally put the throat lash through the ends of the reins and put the nose-band right round the outside of the cheek-pieces. If there is a curb chain, twist it flat and hook it round the front of the bit.

Then hang the bridle up on to the bridle hanger, which should be screwed to the tack room wall, and place the saddle on the saddle peg or saddle rack alongside. The stirrup irons should be hung underneath, and the girths, stirrup leathers and martingale should be hung alongside.

Always clean tack thoroughly after use, so that it will be clean and ready to do justice to you, and your horse, when you set out on your next ride.

What can be learned at a horse show?

One of the better ways a beginner can learn to judge why certain horses and ponies are preferred to others is to spend time as a spectator at horse shows. Whether an international spectacular or a 'local' show, this is the place where you find a cross-section of the equestrian world.

Classes will be held for the smallest of ridden ponies, and for well-turned out hunters. Others will be competing in the jumping competitions or being shown in 'in-hand' events.

But it is at the showing rings where we can learn the most. Watch, for example, a hunter class being judged – and watch every minute and every horse competing. First, there will be a preliminary round in which the hunters are asked to jump a short course of natural-looking obstacles. After all, hunters must be able to jump! In most cases only those with clear rounds will go through to the final judging stage.

Competitors in a Leading Rein class are asked first to walk round the Judges who stay in the centre of the ring. Note how slackly the leading rein is held.

When the final stage comes to be judged the spectator has much to look at. The hunters, having been brought into the ring, will be told to trot, canter and gallop round on both reins. They will then be brought into the centre of the ring. The order of line-up at this point does not necessarily signify the final placings, though sometimes this is the way they finish up!

The Judge will now ride each hunter, again at all paces, checking for obedience to the aids he gives and noting the willingness and smoothness of the ride. When all horses have been ridden the Judge will carry out an examination. Here he is looking at conformation and other technical detail. Of course, this is done with the saddle removed. After a final canter round the Judge's steward will bring the hunters in again, now placing them in the final order.

While all this is going on the spectator need not have been lazy!

Open Mind, a most beautiful four-year-old, standing at 17 hands. Belonging to Mr Douglas Bunn, this Hunter has excellent conformation and has won many national and international Championships.

From the side of the ring you can make your own judgement and order. Select the type you would like to see as champion, and then ask yourself why it was not chosen by the Judge! Look at the way the horses are turned out when they first come into the ring. Look at their paces and general well-being. Then watch the first line-up, trying to assess why certain hunters are placed higher than others. Watch closely as the Judge rides each hunter. Notice the way he will judge conformation. Try to work out the 'sort' he likes.

Of course, you will be at a disadvantage, for the Judge will have had many years of experience and will have had the opportunity of riding each horse and examining it at close quarters. But you can still have fun trying to match his placings! And you will be learning a great deal at the same time.

What is the Pony Club and what are its objects?

The Pony Club has its headquarters at the National Equestrian Centre, Stoneleigh, Kenilworth, Warwickshire. It was founded in 1929 and is today the largest association of riders in the world.

The Pony Club is represented by over 1500 branches all over the world and has a membership in excess of 100,000.

The objects of the Pony Club are to encourage young people to ride and to learn to enjoy all kinds of sport connected with horses and riding, to provide instruction in riding and horsemanship, to instil in its members the proper care of their animals and to promote the highest ideals of sportsmanship, citizenship and loyalty, thereby cultivating strength of character and self-discipline.

Membership is open to boys and girls up to twenty years of age. Not all of the members own their own ponies, and rallies and other

A sack race is not the easiest of events, especially when you have to hold on to your pony! This young lady, wearing her badge and tie, is enjoying a gymkhana event at a Pony Club show.

events are planned to meet the requirements and enjoyment of the non-pony-owning member.

Working rallies, horseshows, one-day events, inter-Branch activities, filmshows, quizzes and other events are held during the year. In the United Kingdom there are 320 branches of the Pony Club with more than 45,000 members. In countries overseas there are now some 1200 branches with 60,000 members. Young people who wish to join and who would like to wear the PC tie and badge should approach their local branch or write directly to the Headquarters at the address given above.

A yearbook is produced, together with many invaluable books of guidance and instruction.

What is the BHS?

The British Horse Society (BHS) is the responsible body, under the British Equestrian Federation, for equitation and horsemastership, guarding the interests of horses and riders and developing riding for recreation and sport, encouraging the care and welfare of horses and ponies and promoting the interests of horse and pony breeding. It is the parent body of the Pony Club and of all affiliated Riding Clubs, providing instruction for their members in riding and the proper care of animals.

The headquarters of the BHS is at the National Equestrian Centre, Stoneleigh, Kenilworth, Warwickshire.

Apart from its work related to Combined Training, Dressage, Eventing, Combined Driving, the Pony Club, Riding Clubs, and Training and Development, the granting of degrees of approval to Riding Schools, the Society is working to expand and improve riding facilities all over the country with the help of bridleway associations and national organisations concerned with the preservation of the countryside.

Glossary

Bandages These are used on the legs and tail, mainly as a protection.

Barns Various types of barn are used for the storage of hay and straw. In America the word can refer to a stable.

Bedding This may consist of straw, sawdust, wood shavings, peat, dried bracken or shredded paper.

Bit The bit, which forms part of the bridle, is used to regulate the pace and direction of the horse, and to raise, lower and draw in the position of the head.

Bitless bridle Sometimes known as a hackamore, this is a bridle without a bit, which acts on the chin and nose carriage.

Bog spavin A puffy swelling on the inside and slightly to the front of the hock.

Bone spavin A bony growth below the hock joint.

Bridle A bridle is used to help control the movements of a horse by exerting pressure on various parts of the horse's head. These include the lips or corners of the mouth, the tongue, the bars of the mouth, the curb groove, the nose, the poll and the roof. There are six main types of bridle, the snaffle, double bridle, pelham, kimb-lewick, gag and bitless.

Bridoon A small snaffle bit used with a double bridle.

Bruised soles Bruised soles are usually caused by a stone and may result in temporary lameness. The sole becomes tender and may show a red mark.

Brushing boots These are usually made of leather or felt with a padded portion running down the inside of the boot to protect the joints if a horse strikes one leg with another.

Capped hock This is a swelling on the joint of the hock usually caused by shortage of bedding or injury when travelling.

Cavesson This word can either mean a cavesson nose-band which forms part of the bridle or a breaking-in cavesson which is a form of headcollar with a padded nose piece.

Clenches This is a term used to describe any protrusion of the nails holding the shoe on to the hoof.

Clipping This describes the removal of part or all of a horse's coat in the winter to enable the horse to cool and dry more quickly after fast work. There are various types of clip including the full clip, hunter clip, blanket clip and trace high clip.

Colic This is a painful disease of the digestive organs.

Condition A term used for the looks and health of a horse or pony.

Corns These are discolourations of the sole of the foot in the region of the heel, usually caused through undue pressure by a shoe.
Cracked heels An inflammation of the skin in the hollow of the heel.
Curb chain A chain which lies in the groove of the jaw just above the lower lip when fitted to a curb or pelham bit.
Day rug Usually of wool with the owner's initials in the corner and with a fillet string which passes beneath the tail and just above the hock to prevent the rug from blowing in the wind.
Double bridle A weymouth or double bridle has an additional pair of reins as well as an extra head strap and cheek-piece, to which is fastened a bridoon.
Dressage A series of gymnastic exercises to show the obedience of the horse to its rider's aids and commands.
Droppings The term usually used to refer to a horse's dung.
Dropped nose-band A nose-band which assists the action of a snaffle bit and prevents a horse from opening its mouth too wide or the bit from sliding to one side.
Electuary The name given to a medicine in which the drugs are made into a paste with a base of treacle or honey, usually used for sore throats.
Fodder The term fodder, or forage, is used to describe any foodstuff normally fed to horses.
Fodder room A room used for the storage of a horse's food, usually kept in sacks or bins.
Forging This is when the hind shoe strikes the fore shoe when a horse is trotting, usually when it is uncollected or being ridden in a slovenly manner. It can also refer to the making of a horse shoe.
Frog This is a V-shaped formation in the sole of the foot.
Gag This is a bit which has rounded leather cheek-pieces passing through the holes in a bit ring for the principal purpose of raising the horse's head.
Gig A two-wheeled carriage to seat two people.
Girth A wide band made of leather, nylon, string or web, used to hold the saddle in place. The name is also used to describe the circumference of a horse's body.
Girth gall A troublesome sore in the area of the girth.
Grazing This is used to describe horses or ponies which are feeding on grass.
Groom Someone who looks after the welfare of the horse.
Grooming The act of getting a horse or pony clean.
Hackamore A type of bitless bridle.

Hand The measurement by which the height of a horse or pony is calculated – 10 cm (4 inches).
Hay net A thick corded net in which a horse's ration of hay is placed and then hung from a ring in the stable or box.
Headcollar Used for leading an unbridled horse or pony or for tying up in a stable or stall.
Hogging A term used for removing the mane.
Hoof The horny covering of the foot from the coronet downwards.
Hoof pick A steel implement for removing dirt and stones from the hoof.
Horse blanket A thick blanket used under a night rug in cold weather.
Horse box Motor vehicle designed for transportation of horses.
Horse trailer An enclosed trailer to carry one, two or three horses, usually towed by a Land Rover or car.
Kimblewick A straight bit with a short cheek-piece and curb chain used with a single rein.
Knee-caps A felt covering to protect the horse's knees during working exercises or when travelling.
Knee spavin A bony growth at the back of the knee.
Laminitis Inflammation or fever of the feet, usually caused by fast work on hard ground or too much eating food without enough exercise.
Lip strap A thin leather strap which holds the curb chain in place.
Loose box Form of stabling which gives freedom of movement.
Manger A feed container usually made of iron or hardwood and fastened to the wall of a stable or stall at a suitable height.
Martingale A leather device to regulate the horse's head carriage. There are three main types – standing, running and Irish.
Mounting block A low platform on which a rider stands when mounting a horse.
Mud fever Inflammation of the heels, legs or belly.
Mucking out The process of cleaning a horse box or stall and removing the droppings.
Muck-heap The name frequently given to a manure heap.
Navicular A disease of the navicular bone, usually confined to the forefeet.
New Zealand rug A weather-proof canvas rug, usually used on horses turned out in winter.
Night rug A jute rug, partly or fully lined, used to keep horses warm at night.
Over-reaching When the toe of the hind shoe strikes against the

heel of the forefeet.

Over-reach boot A circular rubber boot used to prevent injury to the coronet when a horse over-reaches.

Paddock An enclosed area of grassland used for grazing horses or ponies.

Pelham A bit with a double rein and curb chain designed to do the work of a double bridle.

Pincers An instrument used by a blacksmith.

Plaiting The process of putting plaits into a horse's mane or tail to improve the appearance.

Pritchel A pointed metal tool used by a blacksmith to carry a hot shoe.

Puller A horse which pulls, usually through having had its mouth ruined.

Pulled mane or tail When the hair from the underneath of the mane or the side of the dock is removed by pulling to give a tidy effect.

Pulse A horse's pulse is normally 36 to 40 beats to the minute. It is usually taken at the submaxillary artery under the jaw.

Roadwork Exercising a horse on the road to get it fit.

Roller A form of girth made of leather, webbing or hemp to keep a rug in place.

Rugging up A term used for putting rugs on a horse.

Saddle Usually made of felt or leather, attached to the horse's back by a girth to provide support for the rider.

Saddle-horse A wooden stand upon which saddles can be placed for cleaning or storage.

Saddle soap A specially prepared soap which is applied with a damp sponge for cleaning saddles, bridles and other leather harness.

Saddle-tree A frame upon which a saddle is built.

Shoeing The art of making and fixing a shoe on to a horse's foot.

Side bone A hard lump on the coronet on either side of the heel.

Side reins Reins attached to the roller for training purposes or when lunging a young horse.

Side saddle A saddle, usually used by women, when the rider sits sideways on a horse.

Skip A wicker-type basket or metal container used to collect droppings in a stable.

Snaffle fit A bit needing only one rein, which usually consists of a single-jointed or unjointed mouth-piece.

Splint A small bony growth between the splint bone and the canon bone.

Stall A compartment for a horse in a stable in which a horse must be tied.
Stirrup iron A metal fitting in which the rider's foot is placed.
Stirrup leathers Leather straps which are used to attach the stirrup irons to the saddle.
Summer sheet Usually made of cotton or linen to keep away flies and dust from a horse's coat in summer.
Sweat sheet A rug, rather like a string vest, which is used to help cool a horse when hot.
Sweet itch An irritable condition of the skin at the crest, withers and croup in summer.
Tack The name given to describe the saddlery used on a horse or pony.
Tack room A room used for the storage of saddlery.
Tail guard Made of leather or felt and covers the dock completely to prevent any damage to the tail when the horse is travelling.
Temperature The normal temperature of a horse is 38°C (100·5°F).
Tendons Fibrous structures forming bands and cords attaching the muscles to the bones of the legs.
Tendon boots Specially designed boots, usually of leather, which protect the tendons.
Tooth rasp A special file for removing the sharp edges of a horse's teeth.
Trimming Tidying the hairs of a horse's head, mane and tail.
Wisp A pad made of rope, hay or straw, used for toning up a horse's skin.
Wither pad A pad made of soft material placed under the saddle to prevent undue pressure on a horse's back, particularly when the saddle does not fit well.
Wolf teeth Rudimentary teeth in front of the upper and lower molar teeth.
Worms Parasites which can affect the condition of a horse.
Warbles Lumps in the region of the saddle caused by the warble fly.